Introduction to Management

HARPERCOLLINS COLLEGE OUTLINE

Introduction to Management

Claudia Rawlins Däumer, Ph.D.
California State University at Chico

HarperPerennial
A Division of HarperCollins*Publishers*

To Elizabeth Oser Rawlins,
Thanks for your special friendship.

An American BookWorks Corporation Production

Project Manager: Mary Mooney
Editor: Robert A. Weinstein

LIBRARY OF CONGRESS CATALOG CARD NUMBER 91-58273
ISBN: 0-06-467127-5

92 93 94 95 96 ABW/RRD 10 9 8 7 6 5 4 3 2 1

Contents

Preface

As with all of the books in the HarperCollins College Outline series, this *Introduction to Management* is a summary of the topics essential to the first course in a particular field—in this case, to a course in organizational management. Almost all of the topics in a standard management textbook are addressed here.

You can use this book, along with an assigned textbook, to help clarify management concepts. The book offers clear definitions of key management topics and provides many examples of the principles as they are applied in organizations. Different levels of headings, and boldface and italic type make the book handy for review and exam preparation.

On the other hand, *Introduction to Management* is complete enough to serve as a stand-alone text, either for classroom or self-study. What it does not include from a standard textbook are the support materials: cases, review questions, pictures, interviews with managers, and so on.

As a student of management, you need to learn the vocabulary of managers. In *Introduction to Management*, terms are clearly defined. Examples make the terms and concepts come alive. As a beginning student of management, you also need a firm foundation in the kinds of issues and concerns with which managers deal. Planning, organizing, and motivating, for example will be described. This book is about *management*.

What this book is not is a "how-to" book about *managing*. A beginning text cannot answer specific questions about how to manage people and things. Question like, "How do I know when my employee is over-stressed?" or "What if I just don't like one of my employees?"—questions about the active practice of managing—are addressed in more advanced management courses.

Many people helped me as I wrote this book, and I would like to mention them to you. Fred N. Grayson and Mary Mooney of American BookWorks Corporation were patient beyond anything that should have been expected of them. Jonathan Goodrow and Dr. Hans Däumer read the manuscript and provided many helpful comments. In spite of the dedicated help of these four people, I take responsibility for any errors or awkwardness which remain.

My family and friends did a monumental job of remaining supportive while I got increasingly absorbed by this project. Many thanks to all these wonderful people.

And best of luck to you in your study of management. Making organizations work better is an important social, as well as personal, goal. We will all benefit if you can help the organizations of which you are a part use resources wisely and efficiently.

Claudia Rawlins Däumer, Ph.D.
September 1991

1

An Overview of Organizations, Managers, and Successful Management

When people work together, they can accomplish more than when they work separately. However, some groups are more successful at achieving their goals than other groups. The field of management explains why some organizations succeed and others fail.

This book is about how managers can best help their organizations set and achieve goals. All organizations, from bridge clubs to neighborhood grocery stores to multinational corporations, have managers. However, in formal organizations, which provide goods or services to customers or clients, the role of the manager is the most visible and well defined. As a result, our focus will be on formal organizations.

ORGANIZATION DEFINED

Organizations are a necessary element of life: they enable us to accomplish things that we could not do as well—or at all—as individuals. In addition, they serve society and they help provide a continuity of knowledge.

Informal Organization

Informal organizations are groups that emerge spontaneously whenever people interact with one another over time. They exist, for example, at the scene of an accident, on the neighborhood baseball diamond, or in the church choir. They also exist within all but the smallest formal organizations. (chapter 15 discusses the informal organization in greater detail.)

Formal Organization

Management is are part of what we call a formal organization. A formal organization is defined as "a group of people whose activities are consciously coordinated toward a common objective or objectives." All complex, formal organizations, whether they are profit (IBM) or nonprofit (Boy Scouts of America), public (Medicare) or private (Hartford Insurance), share a number of characteristics in common.

1. They all transform resources. The resources can be primarily natural materials. For example, Alcoa transforms bauxite into aluminum. The resources can be primarily labor. For example, Word Pro uses skilled typists to transform handwritten manuscripts into typed documents. The resources can even be primarily information. Tax accountants transform information on tax laws and the client's business into filed tax forms. Historically, the United States' economic system has changed from an industrial, natural resource focus to a service, labor-intensive focus, and most recently, to an information analysis focus.

2. They all interact with and are dependent on elements of the environment external to them. Organizations operate within a society of culturally accepted values and needs. Those values and needs, combined with economic conditions, customers, labor availability, government regulations, competition, technology, and other factors, limit the choices available to organizations. (Chapter 3 provides additional detail about limiting conditions external to the organization and chapter 4 discusses in greater depth the limiting factors within the organization.) Scarce resources place greater pressure on organizations. Foreign markets and international competitors are enlarging the environment within which modern organizations function.

3. They all incorporate a horizontal division of labor. A large job is divided into many specialized small tasks. For example, a doctor can serve many more patients if a receptionist answers the phone and makes appointments and if a physician's assistant performs the preliminary tests of temperature, blood pressure, and urinalysis. Each member of the health team specializes and in so doing makes the whole team more effective and efficient.

4. They all subdivide, often into departments or divisions. General Motors Corporation has divisions for its different product lines. The Cadillac division is separate from the Chevrolet division. Even small organizations often subdivide by activity or function. Manufacturing, sales, and customer service are often located in separate departments.

5. They all incorporate a vertical division of labor. The coordination of work is separated from the performance of work. The tasks necessary to coordinate the work of others are the essence of managing.

MANAGEMENT DEFINED

In the broadest terms, management is defined as "the process of planning, organizing, leading, and controlling the efforts of organizational members and of using all other organizational resources to achieve stated organizational goals." This definition includes several important elements.

1. First of all, management is a process—an ongoing interaction. Taking a snapshot photograph of an organization only tells you where the organization was at the time. By the time the photograph has been developed, the character of the organization and what its managers are doing has already changed.

2. Second, managers use all the resources of the organization. People are the most basic resource of any organization, but managers would be limiting their achievements if they did not also rely on the other available organizational resources. For example, a manager who wishes to increase manufacturing output might not only try to motivate the workforce, but also to modernize the assembly equipment, thus using both human and financial resources to attain the goal.

3. Finally, the definition stresses that management involves achieving the organization's "stated goals." Managers of any organization try to attain specific ends. Perhaps the most significant element in what makes organizations differ from one another is that each organization has its own unique set of goals.

MANAGERS DEFINED

Different authors have used different approaches or models for categorizing what managers do and the skills they need to be good managers. Because managers are active participants in organizations that are constantly changing, each of the views points to different facets of the nature of managing and managers.

Attributes of Managers

Our working definition describes managers as organizational planners, organizers, leaders, and controllers. Actually, every manager takes on a much wider range of roles to move the organization toward its stated objectives. The following is a list of what managers do.

Managers work with and through other people. They act as channels of communication within the organization. They also interact with individuals outside the organization—customers, suppliers, the press, and so on. As a result, good interpersonal and negotiating skills are essential to good managing.

Managers are responsible and accountable. Managers are responsible for seeing that specific tasks are done successfully. Their managerial performance is typically judged by how well they arrange for these tasks to be accomplished. All members of an organization are accountable for their particular tasks. What makes managers different, however, is that they are held accountable not only for their own work, but for the work of others as well. As a result, managing is sometimes especially stressful.

Managers balance competing goals and set priorities. Every manager faces a number of competing demands for time and resources. Because these are always limited, each manager must set priorities. As a result, managers need to be able to see the larger picture, and to manage their time, not getting bogged down in the details of immediate crises.

Managers must think analytically and conceptually. These two thinking styles are almost opposites, requiring managers to use both brain hemispheres in processing information and making decisions. Analytical thinking requires the manager to break a problem down into its constituent parts, analyze those components, and come up with a solution. Conceptual thinking, sometimes called synthesis or synthetic thinking, requires the manager to think about a problem in relation to its larger implications—to see the whole pattern.

Managers are mediators. Organizational members sometimes disagree about how to reach organizational goals or even which goals to reach. Good managers have the listening skills necessary to help mediate such conflict.

Managers are politicians. In order to work with and through people, managers develop networks of relationships and build alliances and coalitions.

Managers are diplomats. They frequently serve as official representatives of their organizations in the community, with clients, customers, government officials, and representatives of other companies. They also represent those they supervise with other managers in the company.

Managers are symbols. They "stand for" the organization. Their manners, the clothes they wear, the cars they drive, and so forth are seen not only as personal symbols, but as symbols of the organization as well. A manager in jeans driving an old car can symbolize the organization's not doing particularly well, or perhaps that the organization is an open, unpretentious, practical one.

Managers make difficult decisions. Nearly all decisions or solutions to problems have negative, as well as positive, consequences. Good managers have the personal confidence and professional commitment to make decisions even when some of the outcomes are unpopular.

Managerial Roles

According to Rosemary Stewart's 1982 research, managerial jobs are alike in that they share three major characteristics—demands, constraints, and choices. Demands refer to *what* has to be done, constraints are the internal and external *limits* within which a person must manage, and choices refer to *how* to do what has to be done. Each managerial job has its own "fingerprint," or unique combination of these three characteristics.

In 1973, Henry Mintzberg studied the work of male executives and concluded that managers play a variety of roles, or display organized sets of behavior, within the organization. In Mintzberg's view, the manager's position, with the authority and status conferred upon it by the organization, creates a kind of human information processing system that we call a manager. Authority and status give rise to interpersonal relationships that lead to inputs (information), and these in turn lead to outputs (information and decisions). He identified the following interdependent roles.

INTERPERSONAL ROLES

Figurehead. The attributes of symbol and diplomat are incorporated in this role.

Leader. This role involves directing others.

Liaison. The liaison role deals with the significant web of relationships that the manager maintains with individuals and groups outside the organization.

INFORMATION ROLES

Monitor. In order to keep the organization on track in reaching its objectives, the manager must obtain information about how the organization is doing—the quantity and quality of work being done.

Disseminator. In addition to obtaining information, the manager shares information with others.

Spokesperson. Managers speak on behalf of their unit, and of those they supervise, to others outside the unit.

DECISIONAL ROLES

Entrepreneur. Managers seek to improve the functioning and accomplishments of their organizations.

Disturbance handler. If the entrepreneurial role is distinguished by managers' voluntarily initiating activities to improve performance, the disturbance handler role, in contrast, features managers' reacting to often unforeseen disruptions that interfere with normal or expected performance.

Resource allocator. Making decisions about how limited time, money, materials, labor, and other resources will be applied to multiple and competing claims upon them is the work of the resource allocation role.

Negotiator. Negotiating is on-the-spot bargaining and exchanging in which the manager is present and agreements are made. It includes the attributes of politician and mediator.

Managerial Levels

The extension of vertical division of labor results not only in managers and workers, but in levels of management. Generally, organizations assign titles to differentiate the levels of managers, but titles are not always uniform and certainly not always indicative of level. For example, the Secretary of the Interior has remarkably different administrative duties from the President's secretary. Regardless of the number of levels within an organization, managers are generally classified into three categories. Sociologist Talcott Parsons defined these levels as technical, managerial, and institutional; they are most frequently referred to as supervisory, middle, and top-level management.

SUPERVISORY MANAGERS

Supervisory, operating, technical or first-line managers represent the level of management immediately above nonmanagerial workers. Supervisors spend the majority of their time monitoring and assisting their subordinates. They focus on the final details of ensuring that organizational goals are met and policies followed. Supervisors must have good technical skills as well as good human relations skills.

It is common for supervisors to feel overwhelmed by paperwork and the number of contacts they must carry out. Supervisors also complain of an identification problem. They sometimes feel they are positioned between management and employees and are really not either.

MIDDLE MANAGERS

Middle managers oversee and supervise the managers below them. Middle managers' jobs vary greatly from one organization to the next, and different organizations have varying numbers of levels of intermediate, "middle" managers. Middle managers serve as a conduit for information and communication between first-line and top-level managers. Effective middle managers have strong human relations and administrative skills.

As computers take over many information processing functions, many organizations are laying off middle managers. According to the Association of Outplacement Consulting Firms, 20,000 middle managers were dismissed from companies in 1985. Since 1980, U.S. companies have shed half a million managers. A March 2, 1987 *Fortune* article reported that even as the economy entered its fifth consecutive year of expansion, an unprecedented wave of shrinkings and realignments, part of the restructuring of corporate America, resulted in tens of thousands of managers being let go. A January 1, 1991 *Fortune* article reported that the recession of 1990–1991 would be led by white collar layoffs.

TOP-LEVEL MANAGERS

In all organizations, the highest organizational level, institutional or top management, has the fewest members. Those who occupy the highest level management jobs tend to have the broadest responsibilities and widest network of interactions, typically requiring them to spend substantial amounts of time with outsiders. Human relations skills and conceptual thinking skills are critical to effective top-level managers.

The top manager, or chief executive officer (CEO), is ultimately responsible for the success or failure of the organization. The top manager's job is open-ended—the job is never done, for as the environment changes, the potential for failure is always present.

*T*he *image sometimes created of management is that it is a rather contemplative activity carried out in genteel tranquility—well ordered, well planned, and well controlled. The reality of managing is that it is highly fragmented and very emotional. Managers spend about 80 percent of their time working with and through other people, assisting their organizations to effectively and efficiently reach organizational goals. As organizational goals change and as environmental opportunities and constraints change, managers use a variety of technical, human relations, administrative, and conceptual thinking skills.*

All formal organizations transform resources, interact with and are dependent on the environment, and incorporate horizontal and vertical division of labor. And all of them require managing.

Selected Readings

Drucker, Peter. 1988. "Management and the World's Work." *Harvard Business Review* 66: 65–76.

Hales, Colin P. 1986. "What Do Managers Do? A Critical Review of the Evidence." *Journal of Management Studies* 23: 88–115.

Helgesen, Sally. 1990. *The Female Advantage: Women's Ways of Leadership.* New York: Doubleday.

Kanter, Rosabeth Moss. 1979. "Power Failure in Management Circuits." *Harvard Business Review* 57 (4): 65–75.

Levering, R. 1988. *A Great Place to Work: What Makes Some Companies So Good (and Others So Bad).* Reading, MA: Addison Wesley.

Levering, R., M. Moskowitz and M. Katz. 1984. *The 100 Best Companies to Work for in America.* Reading, MA: Addison-Wesley.

Miner, John B. 1977. *Motivation to Manage.* Atlanta: Organizational Measurement Systems Press.

Mintzberg, Henry. 1973. *The Nature of Managerial Work.* Englewood Cliffs, NJ: Prentice Hall.

Peters, Thomas J., and Nancy Austin. 1985. *A Passion for Excellence.* New York: Random House.

Peters, Thomas J., and Robert H. Waterman, Jr. 1982. *In Search of Excellence.* New York: Harper & Row.

Steers, Richard M., and Edwin L. Miller. 1988. "Management in the 1990s: The International Challenge." *Academy of Management Executive* 2: 21–22.

2

Historical Perspectives on Managing

*M*odern managers face many new, confusing, and often contradictory situations. In order to handle them, managers need to understand not only what is happening, but also why it is happening. The why can best be understood when placed in a historical perspective.

Managers search for patterns in the problems they face, and they tend to repeat solutions they've used in the past when patterns recur. Experienced managers have more experiences to draw upon than less experienced managers, but no manager has enough personal experience to deal with every problem. A review of the evolution of management thought will help with understanding the patterns in today's organizations. A successful manager needs to know what worked before, and what did not work. Understanding history helps in identifying common themes that seem to recur, and in knowing which solutions to try and which to avoid.

A look at management history will also serve as a reminder that the science of management is in process. It is still developing, and there is much left to understand.

PREINDUSTRIAL ERA

The need to manage complex projects is as old as humankind. Five thousand years ago, Egyptians established supplies inventories, kept sales ledgers, and paid taxes. They developed elaborate organizations for large-scale agricultural and construction projects.

The Old Testament of the Bible suggested vertical division of management and a narrow span of control as appropriate for coordinating the move of a nation's people. The Romans applied coordinated effort to build roads and walls. They developed a factory system for manufacturing and formed guilds—the precursors of labor unions.

In *The Republic*, the Greek philosopher Plato, born in 428 B.C., realized that leading was much more a matter of asking the right questions than of giving answers. He also recognized that entrepreneurial start-ups might require a leadership style different from that required by their successor core businesses.

The Chinese had developed an international trade route for silk by 300 B.C. By 100 B.C., they had sailed as far as India and established trading partners there.

The Renaissance in Europe was accompanied by an awareness of the need for managerial principles. Niccolo Machiavelli wrote *The Discources* in 1531, setting out his observations on government and military organization. Later he wrote *The Prince*, in which he advised an aspiring leader to choose any leadership style or tactic necessary to control the negative aspects of people.

Adam Smith, in his 1776 book *The Wealth of Nations*, described the benefits of division of labor. He believed that mass production was the key to prosperity.

The Winchester Rifle Company used the principle of interchangeable parts in their gun manufacture and, as a result, helped the United States win the Revolutionary War. Eli Whitney extended the interchangeable parts concept to mass production. These people and their ideas are a sampling of the preindustrial contributors to management thought.

CLASSICAL MANAGEMENT THEORIES

In spite of a long history of well-organized groups reaching objectives, management as a *body of theory and principles* is a twentieth century phenomenon. The industrial revolution of the eighteenth and nineteenth centuries gave rise to a need for systematic management. The development of new technologies concentrated great quantities of raw materials and large numbers of workers. Goods began to be produced in large quantity and had to be distributed to widely dispersed users. New technology not only made large-scale operations possible, it made them more economical than small operations. Coordinating the work of many people, machines, capital, and other resources drew attention to the problems of management.

The Industrial Revolution was both the result of and the impetus for a systematic "scientific" look at everything. Managers looking to develop theories of organization, drew from work in anthropology, engineering, mathematics, psychology, sociology, education, and even biology. Between 1880 and 1920, investigation of organizations took two focuses. Scientific Management looked at improving the productivity of individual workers. Classical Organization Theory sought to identify administrative principles that underlie the management of complex organizations as a whole. Together, these two lines of investigation are referred to as Classical Management.

Scientific Management

FREDERICK TAYLOR

Frederick Taylor (1856–1915) built the body of principles which now constitutes the essence of scientific management. He and others sought to determine scientifically the best methods for performing any task and for selecting, training, and motivating workers. He based his managerial system on production-line investigations, wherein he studied and timed the movements of the best workers and then trained the rest of the workers to emulate them. He introduced rest periods during the workday, and paid according to a differential rate system where higher wages were paid to more efficient workers. Thus workers were encouraged to surpass their previous performance standards. He said his philosophy of management rested on four principles.

1. The development of a true science of management, so that the best method for performing each task could be determined

2. The scientific selection of the workers, so that each worker would be given responsibility for the task for which he or she was best suited

3. The scientific education and development of the worker

4. Intimate, friendly cooperation between management and labor

Taylor's methods led to such dramatic increases in productivity that workers and unions began to oppose his approach. They worried that working more efficiently would exhaust whatever work was available and bring about layoffs.

HENRY GANTT

Henry Gantt (1861–1919) worked with Taylor on several projects and then began his own independent work. He suggested that, rather than the differential rate system, workers who completed their day's assignment be given a daily bonus, and that the workers' supervisor also be given a bonus. If all the workers reached the daily standard, the supervisor would receive an additional bonus, encouraging the supervisor to train workers well. Gantt recorded each worker's daily performance on a public chart, noting in red the days when the worker fell below the standard. Gantt also originated a charting system for scheduling production. The "Gantt Chart" is still in use today.

FRANK AND LILLIAN GILBRETH

Frank (1868–1924) and Lillian (1878–1972) Gilbreth used motion pictures to study the individual movements a worker used to complete a job. They divided each task into the micromovements required to complete it. They labeled these micromovements "therbligs" (Gilbreth spelled backwards with the "th" transposed.) They then identified the most efficient movements for completing a job. One of Frank's motion studies found that the number of motions necessary to lay bricks could be reduced from the then average of eighteen to four, the number still used today. As a result, the number of bricks a bricklayer could place in one day tripled. The Gilbreths believed that motion and fatigue were intertwined. If the motions could be reduced, then fatigue would decrease, and worker morale would increase.

Overview of Scientific Management. The contributions of Scientific Management to increased worker productivity were significant. Many of the methods of Scientific Management continue to be used. The approach has a limitation, however, in that it is based on the assumption that workers are purely rational and interested only in higher wages—if one simply told people exactly what to do to increase their wages, they would do it. However, as managers have discovered, workers have social as well as economic needs, and they do not always behave rationally.

Classical Organization Theory

Classical Organization Theory (sometimes called Administrative Theory) was an attempt to identify principles of effective management that would apply universally to all complex organizations. The technical efficiency of the organization was the focus of this approach.

HENRI FAYOL

Henri Fayol (1841–1925), a French mining engineer, believed that management could be taught once its underlying principles were understood and a general theory of management was formulated. He defined management in terms of five functions: planning, organizing, commanding, coordinating, and controlling. He identified fourteen principles of organizational and administrative effectiveness. The principles emphasize efficiency, order, stability, and fairness. He avoided the word "rules" because he did not want to encourage any idea of rigidity, indicating that in organizational administration, everything is a matter of degree.

Division of Labor. The more people in an organization specialize, the more efficiently they can perform their work. Reduced waste, reduced training time, and increased output result from specialization.

Authority. Authority is the right to give orders and the power to exact obedience. Formal authority (granted to the position) and personal authority (derived from intelligence and experience) should be complementary. Authority carries with it responsibility, the obligation to carry out assigned duties. On the other hand, managers given responsibility need enough concurrent authority to succeed.

Discipline. Discipline results from workers and managers respecting the rules governing activities in the organization. Good discipline is the result of good leadership at all levels, fair agreements, and judicious enforcement of penalties for infractions.

Unity of Command. No individual should have more than one supervisor. When employees report to more than one superior, or receive direction from more than one person, conflicts in instruction and confusion of authority result.

Unity of Direction. Tasks of a similar nature that are directed toward a single goal should be grouped under one manager.

Subordination of Individual Interest to the Common Good. The goals of the organization should take precedence over individual goals. When individual goals prevail over organizational goals, the outcome is conflict.

Remuneration. Compensation for work done should be fair for all employees and for the employer.

Centralization. When power, decision making, and authority are concentrated at the upper levels of the organization, the organization is centralized. When they are dispersed throughout the levels of an organization, the organization is decentralized. The optimum amount of centralization varies depending on several factors, the most obvious of which is size. The larger an organization, the more decentralized the power and decision making should be.

Scalar Chain or Hierarchy. The word *scalar* means ladder. A Scalar Chain is a ladder of authority and communication running from the top of the organization to the bottom, connecting each position. Some organizations have many levels or layers of managers and so are said to be tall. Other organizations have few managerial levels. The Scalar Chain in such organizations is short.

Order. Human and material resources must be coordinated in such a way that everything is in the right place at the right time. People will be most effective in the jobs or positions most suited for them.

Equity. Justice and kindliness should be pursued by managers in all their dealings with subordinates.

Stability of Staff. High employee turnover is not good for the efficient functioning of an organization. Planning will help avoid high turnover.

Initiative. Subordinates should be given freedom and encouragement to solve problems and carry out plans on their own, even though some mistakes may result.

Esprit de Corps. Promoting teamwork will give the organization a sense of unity. Managers are responsible for building harmony and team spirit.

MAX WEBER

Max Weber (1864–1920) was born to a wealthy German family with strong political ties. Weber believed that organizations could become instruments of efficiency if structured around certain guidelines. Weber constructed an ideal type, termed a "bureaucracy," that described an organization in its most rational form. A bureaucracy would incorporate the following elements.

Hierarchical Structure. Similar to Fayol's Scalar Chain, a well-defined hierarchy of authority has positions established and linked by a chain of command in a continuous branching out so that multiple layers exist. Power and authority, which increase as one moves up through the levels of positions in the organization, are essential for rationally controlling the behavior of employees.

Division of Labor. Weber also recognized the efficiency of division of labor. The individual performing the task develops a level of expertise, and new employees can be trained in a narrower task more quickly.

Rules and Regulations. Owners, managers, and workers may come and go in an organization, so a system of stable rules and regulations provides predictability and organizational stability. Rules and regulations serve to restrict decision making and interpersonal behaviors to those actions in the interests of the organization.

Technical Competence. In a rational organization, personnel will be chosen based on technical competence, rather than on friendship, family ties, or other forms of favoritism. Examination or education would be important in personnel selection.

Separation from Ownership. Weber believed that owners were one cause of organizational inefficiency because their decisions would be based more on the goal of short-term profitability rather than long-term production efficiency. When organizational members are not owners, Weber believed, decisions would be based on what is best for achieving overall organizational goals.

Positional or Legitimate Power. Organizations achieve rationality when power and authority are vested in the position and not in the incumbent. Vesting the position, not the incumbent, with power and authority, allows for orderly transition when the person behind the role is promoted, demoted, or transferred.

Record Keeping. Since the rational organization will outlive its members, it is necessary for it to develop a memory. Minutes of meetings, written documents, and financial statements are all essential information for future decisions. Managerial access to information will allow the organization to avoid repeating poor decisions.

MARY PARKER FOLLET

Mary Parker Follet (1868–1933) built on the basic framework of the classical scholars of management. However, she introduced new elements, especially in the area of human relations and organizational structure. Some of her work focused on conflict, which she believed was neither good nor bad. She observed that conflict could be resolved by one side giving in, by one side forcing the other to submit, through compromise—where the two sides split the difference and each gives up something, or through integration. In integration, the conflicting parties take a problem-solving approach and seek the best possible outcome for both sides. She believed that integration would result in discussion and resolution of the issues that originally caused the conflict and as a result was superior to the other methods of conflict resolution.

Follet also hypothesized that no one could become a whole person except as a member of a group. As a result, she believed that control in organizations was essentially individual self-control, so that the individual could remain a member of the group.

CHESTER BARNARD

Chester Barnard (1886–1961) was a practicing executive for New Jersey Bell who wrote extensively on the administration of organizations. He defined an organization as a system of independent individuals who willingly cooperate, who share a common purpose, and who communicate regularly with one another. Perhaps the most interesting of Barnard's observations on organizations was his view of authority. He believed that power and authority rested not in the supervisor, but rather in a supervisor's subordinates who could choose to either accept or reject the supervisor's directives. In Barnard's "Acceptance Theory," subordinates would take direction when the directive or command fell within their Zone of Indifference. Four conditions must be satisfied in order for a command to fall in the Zone of Indifference.

1. The subordinate must understand the communicated directive.
2. The subordinate must believe the directive is consistent with the purpose of the organization.
3. The subordinate must believe the directive is compatible with his or her own personal interests.
4. The subordinate must be mentally and physically able to comply with the directive.

Typically, directives about how a subordinate should complete a work task would fall within the Zone of Indifference, whereas commands about how to vote in a presidential election would not. Barnard was the first of the management theorists to note that in order to meet their personal needs, people form informal groups within the larger formal organization.

Overview of Classical Organization Theory. Much of Classical Organization Theory has endured. The concept that certain identifiable principles underlie effective management and that these principles can be learned continues to provide impetus for the study of management. Some of the specific theories may be inappropriate, however. When business organizations functioned in a relatively stable and predictable environment, the classical principles seemed more valid. Today's organizations must function in a turbulent environment, and flexibility is frequently more important than general principles. Workers today are better educated and desire greater participation in decision making. And sometimes, clearly defined rules, regulations, and authority relationships cause unintended consequences. For example, since rules establish a minimum level of performance expected of employees, a minimum level is what they achieve. Perhaps much more could be achieved if the rules were not so explicit.

Classical theories are mechanistic—that is, the organization is seen as a machine and workers are simply parts to be fitted into the machine to make it run most efficiently. Such a mechanical model of organizations is not supported by observation.

THE BEHAVIORAL SCHOOL

In the 1920s and 1930s, the United States underwent another wave of cultural and social change. People moved from the farms to cities. Women were granted the right to vote. More people had the time and money for leisure activities than ever before. People's values were changing, and these changes had an effect on organizations and their management. Management scholars began placing greater focus on the human element in organizations. In general, the behavioral school drew more from the fields of sociology and psychology, while the classical school was based largely in engineering and physiology.

The Human Relations Movement

Classical Organization Theory was based on a model which viewed humans as almost exclusively driven by economic needs and completely rational in their behavior. The Human Relations Movement had as its underlying assumption a model which viewed humans as driven by both economic and social needs. Thus, the contributors to this body of information focused on workers' social behavior.

ELTON MAYO

Elton Mayo (1880–1949) was a faculty member at Harvard Business School. In 1927, he and his colleagues were called in to see if they could explain some strange results of a 1924 experiment at Western Electric's Hawthorne plant near Chicago. In order to develop a physical environment which would best support the productivity of workers at the plant, managers had divided workers into test groups and control groups. They measured the productivity of each group, and then they varied the amount of light in the test group's area and remeasured output. When the test group's lighting conditions were improved, productivity tended to increase just as expected. But there was a tendency for productivity to continue increasing when the lighting conditions were then made worse. Even the equivalent of moonlight appeared to stimulate more output. To compound the mystery, the control group's output also tended to rise as the test group's lighting conditions were altered. After conducting further research, Mayo concluded that employees would work harder if they believed management was concerned about their welfare and supervisors paid special attention to them. This possibility, that workers who receive special attention will perform better simply because they receive that attention, has come to be known as the "Hawthorne Effect."

Other experiments led Mayo to conclude that informal work groups can have a profound effect on productivity. Study of groups who wired banks of phone lines (such as a PBX board) showed that groups had a clear idea of what constituted a fair day's work, and it was less than what management thought it should be. The work group also considered that a minimum amount of work should be completed. The group expected its members to do the minimum but condemned them for doing more than the fair day's amount. One group went so far as to hit a new group member who persisted in working above the group-established maximum. Good pay and a comfortable work environment do not always lead to higher productivity. A set of interpersonal forces on the job, including peer pressure and self-imposed needs and wants, often affect worker behavior. Sometimes those forces override management's efforts.

Overview of Human Relations Movement. The work of Mayo and his colleagues brought attention to the importance of a manager's style and to the power of informal group processes. The concept of workers as "social man" was a major contribution. However, this concept also failed to explain completely individuals in the workplace. The entire matter of productivity and worker satisfaction turned out to be more complex than was originally thought.

Behavioral Science

Some behavioral scientists believed that what motivates people was more complex even than money and social interaction. Based on their training in the social sciences, behavioral scientists began looking at the complicated issue of what motivates people. This topic is investigated in greater depth in chapter 14, where the concept of "self-actualizing man" is discussed. Abraham Maslow, Chris Argyris, Rensis Likert, Douglas McGregor, and Frederick Herzberg added to our understanding of human behavior in organizations. Describing, explaining, and predicting human behavior on the job, they hoped to build a model of behavior that would always be predictive. So far, this goal has not been achieved.

THE QUANTITATIVE SCHOOL

Management Science, sometimes called Operations Research, got its impetus from the quantitative decision-making tools developed for use in World War II. The complex strategy and tactics employed in World War II encouraged the development of mathematical or quantitative models of behavior. In general, these tools are used to identify a problem, develop a model of the situation, and quantify the variables in the model. Aided by the computer, models can be used to ask "what if" questions. Several computer languages have been developed especially for building simulation models.

Overview of the Quantitative School. The contribution of quantitative techniques has been most impressive in planning and organizing production. By applying Operations Research techniques, quality control, inventory planning and control, and human resource planning have improved significantly. Mathematical models have limits, however. The human factor in an organization is not easily quantifiable, and as research has demonstrated, the human factor is significant.

MANAGEMENT THEORIES UNDER DEVELOPMENT

In spite of the many significant contributions made by observers of organizations, many questions remain unanswered. The theories do not consistently predict organizational reality. A manager can't look at the organization and know just what to do to achieve the organization's goals effectively and efficiently. Management theory is still evolving. The goal in understanding organizations is much the same as the goal in physics—to develop a "unified theory" which incorporates all the observations made of organizations and their management. The approaches which follow offer significant additional understanding of organizations. However, these approaches are still "in process."

Systems Theory

In the early 1950s, biologists and ecologists began noting the interconnectedness of nature. Cells, for example, are surrounded by semipermeable membranes. The processes required to keep the cell alive require input from the environment and produce by-products which are released back into the environment. In other words, a cell cannot live separate from its environment—it is part of an open system. In 1956, Kenneth Boulding developed a "general systems theory," which argued that organizations are like organisms—they are made up of multiple subsystems that interact with each other and with the external environment.

Feedback is the key to system controls. As operations of the system proceed, information is fed back to the subsystems.

In order to survive, an open system must have the ability to adapt to changes in the environment. Because the system interacts with its environment, some of the environmental changes the organization must adapt to are caused by the organization itself.

Another key element of systems theory is that of *flow*. A system has flows or streams of information, materials, and energy into and out of the system.

Current research in Chaos Theory, which studies turbulence in flows, may soon be incorporated into our understanding of organizations as systems. For example, water in irrigation ditches sometimes forms eddies which disturb the flow of water. Hurricanes sometimes form in the flow of air. In organizations, labor unrest or major machine breakdown may randomly and significantly disturb the flow of work. Understanding the order inherent in systems that produce random events might add to our ability to predict organizational outcomes.

Overview of Systems Theory. The implication of systems theory for managers is that all the factors of production are integrated and affect each other. Actions taken to correct a malfunction in one subsystem must be carefully analyzed to avoid disrupting other subsystems. As with physicists, management researchers are seeking the "unified theory" that explains all and incorporates the findings of previous research. Although supporters of systems theory hail it as the eventual integrating development in our understanding of organizations, only time will tell if it will evolve enough to integrate all the other approaches.

Contingency Approach

The administrative and human relations principles identified by management theorists are prescriptive—that is, they tell a manager what to do in order to improve productivity. As managers put the principles to work, they discovered that, although the outcome was usually as expected, sometimes what worked brilliantly in one situation failed miserably in another. For example, Fayol suggests that union is strength, and that it comes from the harmony of the personnel. However, in certain situations, organizations may be more productive if there is discord and conflict. Researchers in the 1960s and 1970s sought to discover additional or intervening variables which might explain why a technique that works in one case will not necessarily work in all cases. This became known as the contingency or situational approach. Essentially, this is the view that the most effective management technique might vary in different types of situations or circumstances.

For example, T. Burns and G. M. Stalker conducted studies in England in 1961 which indicated that appropriate managerial techniques were highly dependent on the kind of task the organization was trying to accomplish. When the task was routine and unchanging, the appropriate managerial approach was to emphasize efficiency, a high degree of specialization, and elaborate control systems. However, when the task was nonroutine and changing, the appropriate managerial approach was to emphasize creativity rather than efficiency and to allow freedom for workers to control their own behaviors rather than relying on rules.

As more and more managerial research was undertaken and the results compared, it became evident that virtually all management functions have some element of contingency or situational variation inherent in them. For example, an organization's appropriate strategic action is often based on where its product is in the product life cycle. In each chapter which follows, the situational variables that appear to influence the quality of a manager's decisions will be discussed.

Overview of Contingency Theory. One result of contingency or situational findings is to make managers wary of those who say they have "the answer." What the contingency approach urges is that we avoid the application of any principle as doctrine and remain open to the pragmatic question of "what works best?" in a particular situation.

Identifying what makes organizations effective and efficient continues to attract the attention of thoughtful management practitioners and researchers alike. Several common themes are developed in the historical approaches considered here, themes which demand further study.

Managers desire to improve decision-making rationality; to achieve effectiveness and efficiency, especially through job design and rewards; to use the human resource properly, especially in terms of manager-subordinate relationships; to interact sensitively with the environment, especially regarding strategic planning and social responsibility; and to determine the extent to which subordinates should participate in decision making.

As organizations, and the people who manage them, face the uncertainty which is resulting from massive global changes in technology, competition, information, markets, and values, historical approaches may be ineffective. However, understanding management history provides a perspective for considering the future.

Selected Readings

Boulding, Kenneth E. 1956. "General Systems Theory—The Skeleton of Science." *Management Science* (April): 197–208.

Gantt, Henry L. 1919. *Organizing for Work*. New York: Harcourt Brace.

George, Claude S., Jr. 1972. *The History of Management Thought*, 2nd ed. Englewood Cliffs, NJ: Prentice Hall.

Gilbreth, Lillian M. 1914. *The Psychology of Management*. New York: Sturgis and Walton.

Keys, J. Barnard, and Thomas R. Miller. 1984. "The Japanese Management Theory Jungle." *Academy of Management Review* 9: 345–356.

Koontz, Harold. 1980. "Management Theory Jungle Revisited." *Academy of Management Review* 5: 175–183.

Luthans, Fred. 1973. "The Contingency Theory of Management: A Path Out of the Jungle." *Business Horizons* June: 62–72.

Ouichi, William G. 1981. *Theory Z: How American Business Can Meet the Japanese Challenge*. Reading, MA: Addison-Wesley.

Taylor, Frederick W. 1911. *The Principles of Scientific Management*. New York: Harper & Row.

Wren, Daniel A. 1979. *The Evolution of Management Thought*. New York: Wiley.

3

The Manager's Environment—External to the Organization

Classical Management Theories focused mostly on factors internal to the organization: span of control, authority and reporting relationships, and work and job design. The external environmental factors, such as competitors, interest rates, population growth, and political climate, received little attention by comparison. Partly, that can be explained by the relatively stable, predictable nature of the external environment. Technology changed slowly, the consumer market grew slowly, natural resources and labor were abundant and cheap. Partly, the focus was on the internal rather than external factors because managers could influence the internal factors directly.

Today, the external environment changes rapidly and continuously. Competition for resources and customers is now worldwide. Technology changes as fast as computer chips will allow.

Organizational Darwinism draws an analogy between organizations and biological organisms. According to this theory, organizations must adapt to changes in their environment in order to survive. In order to help them adapt, managers must become astute observers of the environment. Complicating management's job is the interrelatedness of the external factors.

QUALITIES OF THE ENVIRONMENT

The environment as a whole may be viewed both as a source of information and a stock of resources. Depending on its approach to its environment, an organization faces differing degrees of *uncertainty* caused by a lack of information, and *dependence* on others for vital resources. According to one taxonomy, six environmental factors have been identified as affecting an organization's level of uncertainty and dependence.

Munificence

The environment provides resources or raw materials which an organization uses as inputs to its transformation process. Munificence is the degree to which resources are plentiful or abundant in the environment. When McDonald's first started expanding, inexpensive labor was abundant. Baby boomers were young and looking for part-time employment. McDonald's was experiencing a high level of munificence. As the population aged and fewer babies were born, the environment provided fewer teenage workers. Organizations faced with lean environmental resources must either adapt or fail. McDonald's adapted by hiring elderly workers who had retired from career jobs and sought part-time employment to supplement retirement income.

Dynamism

Some environmental factors are more stable and unchanging than others. Dynamism refers to the frequency with which environmental factors change. When a company is operating in an environment of low dynamism, the techniques it uses to produce and sell products can be routine and recurring. For example, cardboard box manufacturing has changed relatively little in the last twenty years. On the other hand, some companies must operate in highly dynamic environments. Fad products have very dynamic demand properties. And high tech electronics manufacturers face environmental instability which can make products and production methods obsolete in a very short time.

Turbulence

Turbulence is related to dynamism. Dynamism reflects the stability of environmental factors. Turbulence reflects the extent to which environmental factors interrelate. When turbulence is high, organizations must alter their operations to adapt to factors often far removed from their direct market. For example, A-1 Steak Sauce has a demand curve influenced by weather. When pasture land has not received enough rain, farmers slaughter more cows because feeding them is too expensive. When more beef is available, the price of steak goes down. Therefore, more people buy steak and the sauce to go on it.

Complexity

When the factors in an organization's environment are similar to one another, the environment has low complexity. When the environmental factors are dissimilar, the environment has high complexity. A flour mill functions within an environment of low complexity. The raw materials (grains) are consistent year after year, the product line (flour) is small, and the customer demand is highly predictable. On the other hand, a hospital functions in an environment of high complexity. Each new customer requires a different mix of technological and human skills, and demand for services is highly variable.

Concentration

The environmental factors important to an organization can be concentrated in one physical location, or alternatively, can be widely dispersed. The more concentrated the factors, the more efficient an organization can be because transportation costs are greatly reduced. For example, many high tech electronics and computer companies are based in the Silicon Valley south of San Francisco or in Seattle because the highly skilled labor force required is concentrated in these areas.

In a low concentration environment, when resources (or supply) and customers (or demand) are widely separated, an organization must make difficult decisions. Will it be more efficient to ship supplies or end product? Even though customers for U.S. automobiles are widely dispersed, the manufacturing facilities are largely concentrated in the upper midwest because the iron ore used for the steel incorporated in the cars is located there. On the other hand, McDonald's puts its facilities where the customers are rather than where the supplies are. As a general rule, the more costly the manufacturing facility, the more likely a company will choose to concentrate its manufacturing plants near the resources and ship product to the customers.

When both raw materials and customers are widely dispersed and environmental concentration is low, the most efficient decision is likely to be widely dispersed plants. For example, raw materials and customers for paper products are distributed nationwide. As a result, Kimberly Clark, which produces paper products, has factories throughout the country.

Consensus

Some organizations are able to make a niche for themselves where competition is reduced by consensus—there is general agreement in the marketplace that an organization provides a needed service and does it well enough that other organizations support it rather than compete with it. Public transportation systems and sports franchises are examples of organizations that function in environments where competition is low. Other organizations, such as Taco Bell or Kentucky Fried Chicken, function in environments where competition is fierce, where there is no consensus that any particular organization has a hold on the market.

Managers' decisions will be improved if they understand where their organizations lie on each of these dimensions. However, the environment can change rapidly, and the more managers notice changes in any of the dimensions, the better able they will be to make future-oriented decisions.

ENVIRONMENTAL ELEMENTS OR DOMAINS

An organization is influenced by many environmental elements or domains. Elements in the external environment can be divided into those which an organization directly affects or which directly affect the organization—the direct-action environment—and those elements which may not have an immediate impact on an organization, but have long-term influence—the indirect environment. Organizational size, market size, and geographical area in which the organization operates all determine the degree to which elements in the indirect environment impact. The indirect environment is usually more complex and uncertain than the direct.

Suppliers

An organization takes resources from the environment and transforms them. The capital, labor, energy, equipment, and raw materials an organization needs must come from the environment. The relationship between an organization and its network of suppliers is critical to the organization. A dispute with labor, for example, can result in the demise of the organization. Eastern Airlines employees decided they would rather not work at all than work for the management of Eastern. The company declared bankruptcy.

Not only are the *amounts* of supplies critical, but an organization must also be concerned about the *flow* of supplies. "Just in Time" inventory systems reduce the carrying costs of supplies inventories; however, they make a firm more dependent on its network of suppliers. Assembly-line processes are especially dependent on a constant supply of raw materials. Each minute a General Motors assembly line is shut down costs tens of thousands of dollars. When the power went out for three hours at a major university, it took computer personnel four weeks to recover the data that were lost.

Customers

Prospective customers must be identified and satisfied. Organizations have traditionally used advertising and direct sales to develop, attract, and educate customers. The approach was pretty much one of "we have a product; now we need a customer." One of the significant changes in modern organizations is their customer focus. The organization finds a potential customer first and then asks the customer what kind of product the organization should make. A customer orientation is becoming a differential market advantage. Stu Leonard's grocery store has become a symbol of the market power of taking a customer orientation. Because he acts on customer suggestions, his Suggestion Box averages 4000 suggestions per day! The more he acts on customer suggestions, the more customers he has. His sales per square foot of floor space are typically 100 times that of an average supermarket.

Quantus Airlines is offering long-distance travelers special features such as showers in the airport waiting areas. Apple Computer has on its payroll employees whose job is to attend computer-user club meetings and collect information about how "hackers" are using current products and what they would like to see on future products.

Competitors

Other organizations that market similar products or services to the same group of customers are a competitive element in the environment. Some companies are faced with a large number of competitors, while others have relatively few. For example, well over half of computer keyboards are made by one Japanese firm. On the other hand, over twenty major automobile manufacturers offer hundreds of model alternatives. When organizations find themselves faced with direct competition, they try to develop a "competitive" advantage—perhaps lower price or greater reliability or a wider choice of options or more standard features.

Trained Labor

Two characteristics of labor are critical—skill and availability. As the number of people in the population who cannot read grows, many are worried that the next generation of workers will not have the *skills* to perform high tech jobs. Just as important as worker skill is worker *availability*. Demographics, or the study of population statistics, indicates that in the next fifteen years, the number of new workers available will be significantly less than the number of new workers business will require. Firms aware of this trend are rethinking their job designs, incorporating more technology to increase worker productivity, and trying to encourage nontraditional workers to become part of the labor force. Problems of labor shortage are compounded in areas where weather, home prices, or commuting distances make the area less attractive.

Political/Legal Environment

Equal employment opportunity laws, health and safety laws, environmental protection laws, restraint of trade laws, consumer protection laws, equal pay laws, and many more all contribute to the complex legal environment within which organizations operate. Most organizations, no matter what size they are, have legal advisors. Because of the connection between politics and law, many organizations attempt to influence the legal environment through direct lobbying or through industry lobbying and contributing to political campaigns.

The probusiness versus antibusiness sentiment and the political stability of a government are two aspects of the political environment that indirectly influence an organization. One of the reasons the U.S. economy has done so well over the years is the stability of the government and its political process. By contrast, business investment in Lebanon is depressed because of political instability.

Technology

To remain competitive, firms must continually innovate. When technology changes, some firms will rapidly adapt to take advantage of the changes. Others will move slowly and may lose customers. For example, word processing is changing the publishing industry. Several book publishers are offering professors the opportunity to create individualized texts by combining standardized paragraphs, visual aids, and exercises written by a textbook author with as much of their own writing as they choose. The topics can be arranged in any order. Royalties will be paid to each author based on how much of each author's work is used in the final product.

Once a new technology is firmly in place, formerly dominant firms may find it impossible to recover. For example, once photocopying machines became widely used, manufacturers of carbon copy paper found themselves in a rapidly shrinking market. As a result, most companies try to stay at the leading edge of technology through research and development efforts.

Economic Conditions

Changes in economic conditions can dramatically affect organizational operations. The Gulf War and a minor economic downturn in the U.S. in late 1990/early 1991 combined to reduce automobile sales by up to 40 percent. Unemployment climbed to its highest levels in eight years.

Tax law can have significant impact on business. In January 1991, the federal government added a 10 percent luxury tax to purchases of cars, boats, furs, and jewelry costing over a set dollar amount (thirty thousand dollars for cars, one hundred thousand dollars for boats). As a result, U.S. orders for new yachts fell 80 percent by May 1991. Purchasers of million dollar boats now go to the Bahamas or other non-U.S. ports. Many boat dealers have gone out of business.

The complexity of the economic domain increases as the world economy becomes more tightly interconnected. Events on the Tokyo Stock Exchange are likely to set the tone for events on the New York Stock Exchange when it opens many hours later. Fluctuations in the value of the dollar relative to other world currencies has an impact on the balance of trade. When the dollar is weak against the German mark (when one dollar buys only one and one-half marks), U.S. products appear to be a better value to German consumers. On the other hand, if the exchange rate is one dollar for two marks, U.S. products will seem very expensive to German buyers.

Society and Culture

Attitudes, values, and customs combine to define the sociocultural environment. The culture within which a manager makes decisions will limit the solutions the manager considers and will provide an ethical framework for evaluating the quality of the manager's decisions. As an example, if the culture places increased value on reducing pollution, a manager's decision to change product packaging to recycled glass will be seen as a good one, even if it costs somewhat more. Consumers, concerned about dolphins drowned in tuna gill nets, have indicated a preference for more expensive tuna guaranteed "dolphin free." When a culture values something, the value will often be expressed in laws.

Ethics is adherence to society's norms and values. In recent years, the American public has expressed increasing concern over the questionable ethical behavior of managers, dramatically altering many formerly accepted business practices. The sociocultural environment of business has become so important that this book devotes an entire chapter to business ethics and social responsibility.

THE INTERNATIONAL ENVIRONMENT

All of these elements and domains affect all organizations to some degree. However those operating internationally face even more environmental complexity. When an organization begins to do business outside its domestic market, its practices must be modified to take into account differences in culture, economics, laws, and political conditions. Hiring local consultants is almost always a good idea. For example, many fast food companies have tried to make it in the Japanese market. None has been as successful as Kentucky Fried Chicken. Kentucky Fried studied all the customs new Japanese shop keepers follow and made certain that they also followed them. The blessing of the priest was sought. An open house for the neighborhood merchants was held. A statue of the Colonel was placed near the door to indicate reverence for the older man who started the company.

More and more organizations are internationalizing. Some of the factors that have contributed to the expansion of the world market are discussed below.

Lower Production Costs

Lower production costs may encourage some organizations to internationalize. Lower labor costs, for example, have encouraged some producers to move their production plants overseas. Levi Strauss has opened several factories in Hong Kong. Many major companies have their payroll work done in the Phillipines. Production costs can also be reduced by buying raw materials internationally. Japan buys timber from U.S. loggers because our raw wood is cheaper than they can purchase elsewhere.

Import/Export Barriers

Taxes or tariffs are often imposed on products made elsewhere. Such tariffs serve as barriers to imported goods and give a price advantage to locally made goods. One way a company can get around tariffs is to make its product in the country where it wants to develop a market. Nissan produces in the U.S. many of the cars it sells in the U.S. Approximately one-third of the Hondas sold in the U.S. are made here.

Many Whirlpool appliances are made of components manufactured in the U.S., shipped to Juarez, Mexico for assembly, and shipped back to El Paso, Texas for distribution. This strategy allows the manufacturer to take advantage of lower Mexican labor rates while avoiding U.S. import duties. General Motors bought Saab, a Swedish company, so that it would have a foothold in the European Economic Community.

Antitrust Laws

In the United States, domestic firms are limited in how large they can grow within an industry by antitrust laws. When Congress originally passed the Sherman Anti-Trust Act in 1890, its objective was to encourage competition among producers and suppliers. Business practices that encouraged the development of monopolies were made illegal.

Expanding internationally allows an organization to use its strategic advantage, while avoiding antitrust problems. A worldwide market provides companies with expanded opportunities for doing more of what they do best.

New World Markets

Firms are always seeking new customers for their products. Transportation and communication technologies have made it possible and relatively inexpensive to move goods and services around the "global village." Thus, organizations internationalize in order to reach new customers. The opening of China and the Eastern Bloc countries to free market forces and greater international trade is providing literally billions of new potential customers.

As more and more companies internationalize, it becomes difficult to tell where their "home" countries are. For example, Maserati, maker of "Italian" sports cars, is a U.S.-owned corporation, while Coca-Cola derives more than 55% of its revenue from non-U.S. operations. Firestone Tire and Rubber is owned by Bridgestone, a Japanese company. Pillsbury, the owner of Burger King, is really part of a British corporation.

Multinational Corporations

When an organization makes direct investment in foreign countries, it is called a multinational corporation. The sales of some large multinational corporations are larger than the total gross national product of the countries they do business in. As a result, they are in a unique position to do good or harm. This remarkable power is one of the reasons the ethical behavior of organizations and their managers is under close scrutiny.

A typical managerial response to factors in the external environment is to plan for them. Managers monitor the environmental domains, and then develop and implement strategic plans in order to respond to the environment in the most successful way. Strategic planning stabilizes an organization's activities.

However, the factors in the external environment are changing at an escalating rate. Increasingly, what an organization needs is flexibility. Managers are faced with a critical paradox. They must find the right combination of stability and flexibility. Creative solutions are required.

Selected Readings

Galbraith, John Kenneth. 1983. *The Anatomy of Power*. Boston: Houghton Mifflin.

Kelly, Robert E. 1988. "In Praise of Followers." *Harvard Business Review* 66: 142–148.

Ohmae, Kenichi. 1989. "Managing in a Borderless World." *Harvard Business Review* 67: 152–161.

Peters, Thomas J. 1987. *Thriving on Chaos: Handbook for a Management Revolution*. New York: Knopf.

Pfeffer, J., and G. Salancik. 1978. *The External Control of Organizations: A Resource Dependence Perspective*. New York: Harper & Row.

Sheets, Kenneth R. 1990. "Labor's Agenda for the '90s." *U. S. News & World Report* March 19: 36 and following.

Stewart, Rosemary. 1979. "Managerial Agendas—Reactive or Proactive?" *Organizational Dynamics* 8 (2): 34–47.

Toffler, Alvin. 1990. *Power Shift: Knowledge, Wealth, and Violence at the Edge of the 21st Century*. New York: Bantam Books.

Toffler, Alvin. 1981. *The Third Wave*. New York: Bantam Books.

4

The Manager's Environment—Internal to the Organization

Organizations do not exist in a vacuum. As the last chapter addressed, they are open systems operating within larger open systems. However, organizations are also separate from the environment—they have boundaries which they protect.

Chapter 3 addressed the set of constraints outside the organizational boundaries. This chapter considers the conditions that are internal to the organization. Factors such as the kind of technology an organization uses, the way workers are grouped into a structure, the amount of inventory an organization has available, or the size of the advertising budget all affect how an organization adapts to environmental constraints.

Together, constraints and conditions provide a context within which managers make decisions. Every decision a manager makes is both limited by and judged by this two-level context.

ORGANIZATIONAL ADAPTATION

A manager's job is to help the organization adapt to its environment. Many of the activities an organization undertakes can be adjusted or transformed in response to changes in the environment. In 1967, J. Thompson developed a model for thinking about the internal environment of organizations and the techniques they can use for making those adaptations. Essentially, he believed that organizations had a *technological core*, the productive capability that makes them unique. The technological core needs to be protected so that it can function in a predictable and orderly way. The organization can use a variety of *coping strategies* to protect its core from too-rapid changes in the environment.

TECHNOLOGICAL CORE

Technology is the means of transforming raw materials into finished goods. According to Weiland and Ulrich, in their 1976 Organization Behavior, machines, equipment, and supplies are all components of technology, but the most important component is the process whereby raw materials are transformed into desired outputs. In other words, a large part of technology is idea and technique. As a result, organizations that provide services have a technological core just as do manufacturing organizations, because both have processes they use in developing their output. Similar products or services can result from different technologies. For example, General Motors produces cars using automated assembly lines. Ferraris are largely hand built using a team approach. H & R Block provides income tax filing services for large numbers of individual filers by using programmed decision-making tools and employees who typically have little university training. Arthur Anderson & Company provides very individualized tax preparation services using highly skilled Certified Public Accountants.

James D. Thompson, a management researcher, classified the general types of technologies using the following categories.

Long-Linked Technology

Long-linked technology is a series of interdependent tasks that must be performed in a sequence. Moving assembly lines are the classic example of long-linked technology. Brewing beer and then aging, bottling, labeling, packing, and shipping it must all be done in a set sequence.

Mediating Technology

Mediating technology brings together groups who wish to be interdependent. For example, a bank functions because tellers, loan officers, accountants, money managers, and others, each with special skills, work interdependently to handle the different needs of different customers.

Intensive Technology

Intensive technology is used when specific skills, techniques, or services are applied to make a specific change in a specific input. A barber cutting a customer's hair, an accountant preparing a tax return, and a lawyer defending a client are all examples of the application of intensive technology.

COPING STRATEGIES

The technological core is the special process an organization uses to transform input. The application of machines, equipment, and supplies is part of the process. Because the technological core constitutes an organization's competitive advantage, it must be protected from too-rapid changes in the environment. Some of the typical coping strategies organizations use to protect their technological cores include the following.

Boundary Spanning

Some of the people who work for an organization spend a great deal of their time working outside the organization. Salespeople, purchasing agents, lawyers, and market researchers are examples of the kinds of positions organizations can create which open their boundaries to the environment and which do so in a way that coordinates the organizational activities with the environment. As the external environment becomes less certain and more changeable, logic might suggest that organizations would reduce the number of boundary spanners and close the organization off from the environment more. As a matter of fact, the opposite is happening. As the environment becomes less certain, organizations are becoming more dependent on "outsiders."

For example, Pacific Gas and Electric, a major power company on the West Coast, has decided to go out of the hydroelectric dam-building business. Rather than build their own dams, they will contract that business out. They are also downsizing their payroll and personnel departments. Electronic Data Services (EDS) will do much of the payroll work, and consulting firms will be hired to handle personnel recruitment and training. Some companies are sending company employees to work in the plants of their customers. For example, Applied Materials, which makes the machines that etch silicon computer chips, has employees working in the factories of their customers in Japan who produce computer chips. IBM and Microsoft have joint product-development teams. So boundary spanners not only bring information about the organization into the environment, they also bring information about the environment into the organization.

Forecasting

Forecasting is a process of using past and current information to predict the future. The prediction can be based on simple trend analysis or on complicated cause-effect models. The better an organization's ability to foretell its future, the more able it will be to use other coping strategies successfully. McDonald's has information about typical sales for every day of the year, and adjusts raw materials ordering and employee scheduling based on historical information. The company also has data on how local temperature, school holidays, advertising, employment levels, and other factors influence the overall daily sales trends.

Buffering

One of the ways organizations can adapt to and cope with environmental uncertainty is by using inventories—of both inputs and outputs. If an organization has inventories of supplies, changes in the quality and availability of raw materials can be more easily adjusted to. For example, during the Gulf War, retail gasoline prices remained relatively stable, even though both Iraqi and Kuwaiti crude production was disrupted. The U.S. and other countries had large strategic inventories of oil.

Finished goods inventories can also be used to buffer environmental uncertainty. The DeBeers diamond company nearly single-handedly sets diamond prices by controlling the number of diamonds on the market at any time.

Smoothing

Demand for products is not usually constant. However, organizations can take some steps to smooth customer demand. Many restaurants, for example, offer "early-bird" special prices to customers who will eat dinner before 6 p.m. Telephone companies offer lower rates to customers who will call during the night. Power companies offer reduced rates to customers who reduce their peak-time energy use. Smoothing demand allows the organization to use its productive capacity over a longer time period and reduces overtime and layoffs.

Rationing

At least in the short run, the productive capacity of an organization is relatively fixed. However, when an organization produces more than one product, it can shift the focus from one product to another in response to shifts in demand. Paint companies can increase the runs on popular colors and decrease the batch size on colors that are moving slowly. During an emergency, a hospital can shift its resources from less critical patients and procedures to focus them on the emergency situation. In the longer run, organizations can change what they do. Tobacco companies, faced with declining sales, have added other products to their lines. For example, Philip Morris has purchased 7–UP, the soft drink company.

Organizing Structure

One of the ways companies adjust to changes in demand is to adjust their internal organization. For example, a company that produces computer hardware might organize its internal structure by creating three different sales divisions—one for personal computer users, one for corporate computer users, and one for government contracts. Should federal budget cuts grow and substantive global peace treaties receive approval, the computer company might assume that government contracts for hardware would decline. In such a case, the company might better use its resources by reorganizing its sales divisions into a division for small minicomputers and personal computers and a division for large mainframe computers.

As the business environment has changed over the last ten years, more and more companies have added customer service departments and supplied them with substantial budgets. The June 17, 1991 issue of *Business Week* ran a cover story about how IBM's chief executive officer, J. Aker, is trying to move the giant computer company toward a service orientation.

Changing Management

An organization's culture or style is usually the direct result of top management. As the environment changes, a change in style may be called for. Usually the fastest way to achieve a change in style, especially when the organization is in crisis, is to change top management. Lee Iacocca's almost immediate influence on Chrysler Corporation serves as a good example of the power of changing management as a coping strategy. The Soviet Union's rapid changes came concurrently with the appointment of Gorbachev. As internal strife and disappointment over the Soviet Union's slow economic improvement grew, the calls for Gorbachev's resignation grew.

ENVIRONMENTAL CONTROL

In addition to adapting within, an organization can cope with changes in the external environment by attempting to control them. Organizations are taking a more and more active role in attempting to influence the environment. They do this in two major ways: creating favorable linkages, and manipulating the environment.

Creating Linkages

One way to cope with changes in the environment is to establish links with other organizations. The last ten years have seen a record number of mergers, takeovers, and buyouts among U.S. corporations. For example, the *Wall Street Journal* reported in February, 1991 that only 5 percent of the Food Workers Union's 100,000 southern California members work for the same corporate entity that they had five years earlier. In order to reduce international trade restrictions, many companies are establishing mergers. For example, General Motors and Toyota have agreed to produce a car jointly. Ford purchased a major interest in Great Britain's Jaguar, so that the company has an opening into the European Economic Community. Organizations even use membership on their Boards of Directors to establish linkages that might lead to greater information about the environment. Retired high-level government officials and bankers are frequently sought out for directorships because of their "inside" information about important aspects of the environment.

Environmental Manipulation

Not only do corporations advertise their products to customers, but they have also taken up advertising their philosophies. The objective is to influence the regulatory environment, either directly or indirectly. Mobil Oil has taken advertising space in the *Wall Street Journal* since the early 1970s to discuss its corporate philosophy on issues as varied as clear-cutting of forest land to double-hulled oil tankers. Johnson & Johnson responded to the 1983 Tylenol cyanide poisonings by working with the Food and Drug Administration on tamper-proof packaging requirements. Most industries and some individual companies pay lobbyists to represent their interests with governmental decision makers, and they make sizable Political Action Committee (PAC) contributions to the campaign funds of legislators who support their positions.

INTERRELATED VARIABLES

All the coping strategies an organization can use to protect its technological core are interrelated. An organization is an interaction between a social or people component and a technical component. As a result, it is referred to as a sociotechnical system. To some degree, a change in any one of the variables changes the system. Getting new word processors for the secretarial staff is very likely to result in changes not only in the way material is processed for mailing, but in the behavior of the secretaries as well. For many years, production firms focused on the technical component. And for many years, organizations saw themselves as somehow separate from the environment in which they functioned. Modern organizations realize that view is not only inaccurate, it is also likely to be costly. They give careful thought to how they can respond in productive ways.

*A*n organization must indeed react and adapt to the forces of the external environment. Fortunately, it has at its disposal a variety of coping strategies. Some of those involve changing the technological core to take full advantage of new tools, methods, and ideas. The rapid incorporation of computers is an example. Some involve changing the internal organizational structure. Workers can be made part of a team, new departments can be created, new employees can be hired, and inventories can be made smaller or larger. And some involve influencing or changing the external environment. A company's response to losing market share to a competitor can be to buy out the competitor, to increase advertising, or to lobby for import tariffs. It can also be to train its employees to be more efficient and thus reduce labor costs.

The concept of equifinality means that there are many effective paths for getting to the same destination. Different companies can choose different mixes of these coping strategies and all be successful. On the other hand, some combinations of strategies are much more effective, and thus more profitable, than others. It is the manager's responsibility to make high-quality decisions about an organization's best coping strategies.

Selected Readings

Aldrich, H. and D. Herker. 1977. "Boundary-Spanning Roles and Organization Structure." *Academy of Management Review* 2: 217–230.

Drucker, Peter F. 1985. *Innovation and Entrepreneurship: The Practice and Principles.* New York: Harper & Row.

Kotter, J. P. 1979. "Managing External Dependence." *Academy of Management Review* 4: 87–92.

Lewin, Arie Y., and John W. Minton. 1986. "Determining Organizational Effectiveness: Another Look, and an Agenda for Research." *Management Science* May: 514–538.

Stearns, T., A. Hoffman, and J. Heide, "Performance of Commercial Television Stations as an Outcome of Interorganizational Linkages and Environmental Conditions." *Academy of Management Journal* 30: 71–90.

Thompson, James D. 1967. *Organizations in Action.* New York: McGraw-Hill.

5

Social Responsibility and Managerial Ethics

The decisions managers make must further the goals of the organization. Additionally, they must serve the best interests of the society. The traditional ethic of "let the buyer beware" has been replaced with a new concept of corporate social responsibility.

Laws increasingly hold individual managers accountable for the behavior of their organizations. As a result, managers are beginning to look at the long-run consequences of their decisions. They are considering issues beyond "bottom line" and profitability.

Each culture defines "socially responsible behavior" differently. Managers who make decisions with international consequences are especially vulnerable to censure. The more managers understand what is meant by corporate social responsibility and ethical managerial behavior, the more likely they are to meet the expectations of the sociocultural environment within which they function.

THE HISTORICAL ROLE OF BUSINESS IN SOCIETY

Until the depression of the 1930s, most citizens of the U.S. were comfortable with the belief that businesses should focus their energy on making profits. The direct outcomes of this approach were expected to be jobs for workers and a healthy economy. The indirect outcomes of profit maximization were addressed by Andrew Carnegie, in his 1889 book, *The Gospel of Wealth*. He argued that the wealthy hold their money in trust for society. He believed that corporate social responsibility arose from two basic concepts, the charity principle and the stewardship principle.

The Charity Principle

In general, the charity principle holds that those with wealth must assist those without wealth. Looking after those less fortunate than oneself is part of the responsibility that goes automatically with having money. Certainly many are helped through charity. On the other hand, the wealthy themselves decide how much to contribute and to whom. The responsibility for charity falls on individuals, not on the businesses that make them wealthy.

The Stewardship Principle

The stewardship principle holds that the owner of a business is really just its caretaker or steward. In addition to making profits today, the wealthy are to manage their assets such that increasing profits are expected in the future. Power carries with it responsibilities.

In general, Carnegie's approach to social responsibility appealed most to those who were committed to preserving the free enterprise system. Keeping the vehicles of the economic system free from government and social pressure was seen as a valued goal.

However, the Great Depression and two world wars greatly increased the need for social responsibility. Wealthy individuals, doing their best to apply the charity and stewardship principles, simply could not meet the society's needs for social assistance.

APPROACHES TO SOCIAL RESPONSIBILITY

A basic problem underlies all discussion of corporate social responsibility. Precisely whose values are to be supported? The literature provides three very different approaches to thinking about corporate social responsibility issues.

Profit Concept

In 1776, English economist Adam Smith argued in *Wealth of Nations* that the self-interest of private enterprise would result in the greatest good for society. When businesses attempt to maximize their profits, they also promote the public or social interest. According to Smith, they are guided by an "invisible hand" to use society's scarce resources for the greater good of all. Any action not in the best interest of the firm works against the invisible hand and reduces the good to the larger society. If a company makes an unsafe product, the consumer will shop elsewhere, so it is in the company's self-interest to make safe products. If a company pays wages too low, workers will refuse to work there, and the company will lack talented labor.

Nobel prize-winning economist Milton Friedman has expanded on Adam Smith's profit concept of social responsibility, arguing that "the business of business is business." He believes that business organizations that focus on profit and efficiency are fulfilling the role society expects of them, and in so doing, they are being socially responsible. He states that the proper role of business is "to use its resources and energies in activities designed to increase its profits" and shareholder wealth. According to Friedman, business organizations are a collection of people skilled in profit maximization. They do not have the necessary skills for solving social problems. As a result, they should do what they are best at and let others work on social responsibility.

Critics of this approach point out that it is based on narrow thinking and outdated assumptions. For example, it assumes that consumers have perfect information about the company and its products and free access to competitors, and that individual firms have no market power and no control over prices. However, perfect competition is more an ideal than a reality. Critics also point out that often profit for the few is made at the expense of the many. According to a July 6, 1987 *Fortune* article, the richest 1 percent of Americans own 34.4 percent of the national wealth. Less than one-half percent of Americans are millionaires.

Social Power/Social Responsibility

In the 1960s and 1970s, society demanded more social sensitivity from business than it had been delivering. By using the power of law, the citizens extracted certain behavior, especially in the areas of product safety, worker safety, and environmental protection. Management scholar Keith Davis observed that business is subject to an "Iron Law" of social responsibility, which states that "in the long run, those who do not use power in a manner that society considers responsible, will lose it." According to this concept of social responsibility, business is at the mercy of societal constraints. The timber industry has recently felt the Iron Law. Voters in California and Oregon were convinced that logging companies were thinking only short run, cutting down irreplaceable old-growth forests for export. They passed legislation to limit cutting so much that many logging firms have shut down. Business is becoming very sensitive to who votes and who holds political office.

Stakeholder Concept

A broader way of looking at corporate social responsibility is to consider *stakeholders* and their interests. A stakeholder is anyone who has a "stake" or interest in the operations of a firm. Business affects many social and economic stakeholder groups and is affected by these groups in turn.

Since shareholders are the owners of the firm, their stakeholder interests are obviously given a high priority. Shareholders have direct say in who manages a company and how it is managed. However, many other stakeholder groups might be considered by a firm's managers. Consumers have a stake in the safety, quality and availability of the company's products. Employees have an obvious interest in the long-term financial health of the organization, but they also have a stake in the firm's employment and promotion practices, safety record, pay and benefit policies, and training programs. Suppliers have a stake in the firm's product line, its market share, its commitment to contractual obligations, the quality of its long-term planning, and its long-term stability. The government has a stake in the taxes a firm pays as well as its willingness to work within legal constraints. The community in which a firm operates has a stake in the firm. For example, one area of special concern for community stakeholders is a firm's impact on the physical environment. Commuting workers, large paved parking lots, toxic by-products, and noise are likely environmental consequences of a firm's operations. A conscious consideration of stakeholder interests helps managers make socially responsible business decisions.

MANAGERIAL ETHICS

Corporate social responsibility covers an organization's relationships with the external world. Ethics is a more general topic covering both internal and external relationships. Ethics can be defined as the study of how decisions affect other people. Almost every business decision has an ethical component. Ethics includes the study of people's rights and duties and the rules that people apply in making decisions. Ethics is concerned with the principles that define right or wrong conduct.

Business ethics focuses on a wide range of conduct by managers and employees, and is concerned with both the ends and the means to the ends. Because individual values vary, standards of ethical behavior appropriate to entire business organizations are sometimes difficult to agree upon. However, organizational members are expected to strike a balance between economic performance and ethical performance.

Ethical questions may occur at four levels, which are not mutually exclusive.

Societal Level

At the societal level are ethical questions about the basic institutions in a society. Who is best equipped in a society to decide the distribution of goods and wealth: government, the marketplace, or voters? Who should be in charge of educating the children: government, family, or church? What factors determine status and power: wealth, heredity, or age? Questions such as these are rarely permanently answered in a society. Rather they constitute an on-going debate, which individuals can try to influence.

Stakeholder Level

At this level, the ethical questions deal with the external groups affected by an organization's decisions. If a company believes it would be financially prudent to close one of its plants, what does it owe the community or the employees who will lose their jobs? If a company product is helpful to many, but can harm developing fetuses, what responsibilities does the company have? How will such questions be decided? These questions deal with business policy, and managers make such decisions daily.

Internal Policy Level

How should a company treat its employees? Ethical questions surrounding an organization's relationship with its own members are considered at the internal policy level. How much participation should employees have in decision making? What sort of labor contract is fair? In answering questions at this level, organizations have a chance to apply ethical values to themselves.

Personal Level

At the personal level, ethical questions center around how people should treat one another. How direct and honest should they be? How supportive of personal as well as professional concerns? These questions are asked again and again, day after day. And each interaction with others provides an opportunity to demonstrate personal ethics.

THE BODY OF COMMON MORALITY

The real situations individuals face are often fraught with competing interests. Moral rules provide the guidelines that help individuals decide which interest will win out. Ethicists have identified a body of moral rules that cover ordinary ethical problems and refer to these as the "body of common morality."

Promise Keeping

Every moral theory asserts that people should keep their promises. People want some assurance that others will do what they say. Business is based on promise keeping. Contracts are merely formalized promises. When a supplier agrees to supply raw materials, the purchaser is counting on the supplier to keep its promise.

One of the difficulties of international business is that cross-cultural negotiators do not always understand what has been promised and so are anxious over whether promises will be kept or not. A Saudi Arabian was two hours late to a business meeting with an Oregon supplier of computer parts. The American was delighted at how quickly the Saudi signed a two million dollar contract, and was then later dismayed to find the Saudi had no intention of keeping the contract. He signed because he felt badly that he was late to the meeting.

Non-malevolence

Malevolence means harm or ill will. Moral theories require that people treat one another nonmalevolently—that they refrain from harming other people. Trust is necessary to most human interaction. Trust is based on a sense that others will refrain from wishing you ill.

Trust would be impossible if basic physical safety were a constant concern. We are required to avoid using violence to settle disputes. Because force is sometimes believed to be necessary, the guidelines for who can use force and under what circumstances are clearly set out. Police can use "reasonable" force. The military can use force in war situations, but even then we require that they follow set guidelines. When violence breaks out in business, as it did in the Greyhound Bus Lines strike several years ago, management, labor, and customers will have a great deal of trouble trusting each other in the future.

The rule of nonmalevolence can apply to business in issues of worker or product safety. When workers are working under hazardous conditions, law and morality require that the company inform them and fairly compensate them for their risk. When a company's product injures a consumer, the company is under moral obligation to compensate the injured. The original fuel system on the Ford Pinto made it vulnerable to fire in a rear-end collision. Ford has paid millions in liability suits to purchasers harmed as a result of the poor product design.

Mutual Aid

Moral theory requires that we come to one another's aid. People are expected to provide active assistance to each other. Our sense of community comes from the expectation that we will provide mutual aid. In business, this moral rule results in medical benefits for workers, in short-term loans, in employee counseling and other employee assistance programs.

Respect for People

Although not all moral theories include this principle, most common morality requires people to regard others with respect. Respect includes taking others seriously, accepting their interests as legitimate, and regarding their desires as important. Organizations that include employee and customer representatives on the Board of Directors, that act on the suggestions in the employee suggestion box, and that rely on group decision making are putting this moral rule in action. The alternative to this principle is to view others as means to achieving a personal end. It is possible to apply all the previous principles and stop short of this one. Companies that take an adversarial position toward labor and make most decisions autocratically are most likely not applying this moral principle. When a moral theory does not include this principle, it is because the assumption is that each individual will look out for his or her own best interests. In these theories, self-respect is far more important than respect for others.

Respect for Property

As with respect for people, not all moral theory includes respect for property as part of the body of common morality. This principle requires that people get the consent of others before using their property. In the United States, common law supports rights of private property in most situations, so we are more likely to apply this principle than other cultures might be. Typically, employees are not to take company property for their personal use. Timber companies cannot cut trees on someone else's property. Chemical plants cannot dump toxic waste on public lands.

Moral rules for behavior, such as those above, often become internalized and are accepted as values. A *value* is a relatively permanent desire that appears to be good in and of itself, not because it is related to something else.

INSTITUTING ETHICAL BEHAVIOR

A widely held perception is that ethical decline has reached critical proportions in this country. In the past ten years, two-thirds of *Fortune*'s 500 largest corporations have been involved in some form of illegal behavior. While common street crime is estimated to cost four billion dollars per year in the U.S., white-collar lawbreaking is estimated to cost at least forty billion dollars. Executives cite pressures from their organizations for profits as a major reason for ethical decline. Starting at the top, managers and their subordinates must make progress toward seeing the consequences of managerial decisions as long-run issues. Michael Josephson, an international ethics lecturer, says "It is not a matter of being a Goody Two-Shoes. It is a matter of being practical. The notion that nice guys finish last is not only poisonous but wrong. In fact, the contrary is true. Unethical conduct is always self-destructive and generates more unethical conduct until you hit the pits."

Training

Several things can be done to improve ethical performance. One is increasing employee awareness of ethical issues. A growing number of organizations are including ethics training in their employee training and development programs. The training usually includes discussions of real or hypothetical situations. Participants are encouraged to develop alternative ways of dealing with each problem. In their book, *The Power of Ethical Management*, authors Blanchard and Peale suggest that before making a decision that has ethical overtones, decision makers ask themselves how they would feel if their decision were known to their families and/or published in the newspaper.

Support Whistle Blowing

Most unethical behavior is observed by someone. However, the observer must feel safe in order to report the behavior—to blow the whistle on it. Some of the worst ethical violations result from the absence of conscientious naysayers. Calling a boss or an organization to task is high-risk behavior. In many organizations, the messenger bearing bad news is figuratively killed. As a result, top management must unequivocally protect whistle blowers.

Codes of Ethics

A code of ethics is a formal statement of an organization's principles of appropriate behavior. It might address confidentiality, accounting and internal standards, conflicts of interest, employee and product safety, business gifts, and personnel issues. Some codes are very short (Eddie Bauer's is one-half page), and others are quite long and detailed (Chevron's is thirty-one pages.) Many specify clearly the consequences of violating the code. For example, McDonnell Douglas' Code of Ethics is as follows:

"Integrity and ethics exist in the individual or they do not exist at all. They must be upheld by individuals or they are not upheld at all. In order for integrity and ethics to be characteristics of McDonnell Douglas, we who make up the corporation must strive to be:

Honest and trustworthy in all our relationships.

Reliable in carrying out assignments and responsibilities.

Truthful and accurate in what we say and write.

Cooperative and constructive in all work undertaken.

Fair and considerate in our treatment of fellow employees, customers and all other persons.

Law abiding in all our activities.

Committed to accomplishing all tasks in a superior way.

Economical in utilizing company resources.

Dedicated in service to our company and to improvement of the quality of life in the world in which we live.

Integrity and high standards of ethics require hard work, courage, and difficult choices. Consultation among employees, top management, and the Board of Directors will sometimes be necessary to determine a proper course of action. Integrity and ethics may sometimes require us to forego business opportunities. In the long run, however, we will be better served by doing what is right than what is expedient."

Professional Advisors

A growing number of organizations are developing formal positions for people specifically trained to deal with ethical issues. Ombudsmen, employee assistance personnel, and telephone "hot lines" provide confidential outlets for employees. Review committees advise directors and top managers on sensitive ethical issues. Review committees are frequently composed of people from both inside and outside the organization.

Top Management Actions

All the policies, codes, advisors, and training in the world will make little difference if top management is more interested in short-run profits than in ethical and socially conscious behavior. Because many ethical decisions fall in a gray area, clear management direction, in action and attitude, is essential to developing an ethical culture. Decisions build upon each other. Their cumulative effect is the responsibility of top management.

Following Effective Role Models

Business is not without role models of highly ethical behavior. Johnson & Johnson's handling of the 1983 Tylenol poisonings has become a classic in how to handle a difficult situation well. In the Chicago area, seven people died of cyanide poisoning from taking Tylenol capsules. Within hours, all Tylenol products had been removed from the shelves of retailers in the Chicago area. Within three days, Tylenol capsules were removed from the shelves of retailers nationwide. Johnson & Johnson had no reason to believe the cyanide contamination was a result of a production problem, but they believed that retaining customer confidence was of highest priority. The company sent its own research staff to work with Food and Drug Administration officials in identifying the source of the poison. Within days, it became clear that the capsules had been tampered with after they were on the retail shelves and that Johnson & Johnson was in no way to blame.

In spite of having no legal responsibility, Johnson & Johnson offered to buy back all Tylenol capsules from customers who had unused pills. The company established toll-free phone numbers, which employees staffed 24 hours per day to answer questions from concerned consumers. The company held daily news conferences, providing the news media with whatever information was available. Finally, Johnson & Johnson worked with the Food and Drug Administration and Congress to design the tamper-resistant packaging that is now the industry standard. In the short run, Johnson & Johnson's response was very costly. In the long run, consumer confidence in the company's products in general and in Tylenol in particular has come back very strong. Tylenol has regained all the market share it lost.

In contrast, Exxon's handling of the Valdez oil tanker accident in Alaska has hurt the company's image. Throughout, Exxon has argued the legal (as opposed to ethical) issues in court. They have appealed each court decision and argued the limits of their financial liability.

*B*usiness plays an important role in any culture. However, the specific role it plays is the result of society's expectations. Some believe that the only social role business should play is to maximize profits. This view has come to be seen as extreme. Profit maximization in the short run may have too many social costs in the long run.

The society, applying legal and political power, has demanded greater social and ethical sensitivity from business. It has required that business take into account the community of individuals whose lives are affected by its decisions. The power of stakeholder groups who have an interest in the behavior of organizations is growing.

The topics discussed so far all lead to the same conclusion—managers make decisions that impact others. They are part of an interacting system of systems. As a result, the consequences of decisions need to be carefully considered before the decisions are made.

Selected Readings

Blanchard, Kenneth, and Norman Vincent Peale. 1988. *The Power of Ethical Management.* New York: William Morrow.

Carroll, Archie B. 1984. *Social Responsibility of Managers.* Chicago: Science Research Associates.

Davis, Keith. 1974. "The Meaning and Scope of Social Responsibility." In *Contemporary Management*, edited by Joseph W. McGuire. Englewood Cliffs, NJ: Prentice Hall.

Fadiman, Jeffery A. 1986. "A Traveler's Guide to Gifts and Bribes." *Harvard Business Review* 64: 122–136.

Frederick, William, Keith Davis, and James E. Post. 1990. *Business and Society: Corporate Strategy, Public Policy, Ethics.* 7th ed. New York: McGraw-Hill.

Freeman, R. Edward, and David L. Reed. 1983. "Stockholders and Stakeholders: A New Perspective on Corporate Government." *California Management Review* 8: 88–106.

Friedman, Milton, and Rose Friedman. 1979. *Free to Choose.* New York: Harcourt Brace Jovanovich.

Jacoby, Neil H. 1973. *Corporate Power and Social Responsibility.* New York: Macmillan.

Robin, Donald, Michael Giallourakis, Fred R. David, and Thomas E. Moritz. 1989. "A Different Look at Codes of Ethics." *Business Horizons* 32: 66–73.

Staw, Barry M., and E. Szwajkowski. 1975. "The Scarcity-Munificence Component of Organization Environments and the Commission of Illegal Acts." *Administrative Science Quarterly* 20: 345–354.

Wartick, Steven L., and Philip L. Cochran. 1985. "The Evolution of the Corporate Social Performance Model." *Academy of Management Review* 10: 758–759.

White, B. J., and B. R. Montgomery. 1980. "Corporate Codes of Conduct." *California Management Review* 22: 80–87.

6

Creative Problem Solving and Decision Making

Managers make decisions almost constantly. No matter how large or small the decision, each contributes to the fundamental success or failure of the organization. Because the context within which managers make decisions is complex and changing, making high-quality decisions is difficult.

Some decisions are made after painstaking data gathering and analysis; some problems demand instant decision making. In either case, managers can improve the quality of their decisions by learning about the decision-making process and the factors that contribute to high-quality decisions.

In some cases, managers can use decision-making tools like computers to remove part of the burden of being decisive. Even in such cases, the manager remains responsible for the quality of the decisions.

MANAGERIAL PROBLEM SOLVING

Problem solving (or decision making) might be identified as the "core" or essential management function. It is what managers are hired to do. First-line supervisors making hourly decisions about work scheduling and the Chief Executive Officer (CEO) making annual strategic decisions about the long range future of the organization are likely to go through the same processes and experience similar discomforts as they reach their decisions.

New technologies, changing social expectations, a more educated workforce, and other factors are combining to make *creative* problem solving a necessity. New solutions as well as innovative versions of old solutions are required.

Creative problem solving is essentially an eight-step process. Although the process is sequential, in some situations the entire process is completed in seconds. In other situations, several years might be spent reaching a decision. A brief discussion of each of the eight steps follows.

Environmental Analysis

The manager must constantly monitor the environment, looking for information that might indicate a problem is developing. Some organizations collect information systematically using sophisticated computerized Management Information Systems (MIS). Others approach environmental analysis more informally. In either case, the manager is looking for patterns that indicate change. If sales have grown rather steadily each month for three years and last month they fell, is that the beginning of a pattern? John Naisbitt, author of *Megatrends* and coauthor of *Megatrends 2000*, and Alvin Toffler, author of *Future Shock, The Third Wave,* and *Power Shift*, are renowned for their ability to identify emerging patterns in banks of data. Many industries have specialized organizations and journals which keep members aware of issues that might be important to them.

Problem Recognition

Problem solvers rely on their intuition as well as "hard data" to alert them to a possible problem. Managers sometimes have a vague feeling that something has gone wrong or that a new opportunity exists. As an aid to problem recognition, Management Information Systems can be programmed to report when actual figures (of production, expense, sales, and so forth) are significantly higher or lower than budgeted or expected figures. When sales are higher than expected or costs are lower than expected, aware managers are as cautious as when sales are down or costs are high. Perhaps a previously unrecognized opportunity has arisen.

The 3M researcher who developed Post-It Notes was at first very disappointed with his discovery—he was looking for an adhesive that would stick tight. What he developed was an adhesive that did not stick tight—in fact, it allowed paper to be temporarily attached to paper. Once he had observed the qualities of his discovery, he recognized he had the solution for a previously unspoken problem.

Problem Identification

Actually clarifying the problem—separating symptoms from causes—is remarkably difficult and requires careful analysis. Was Saddam Hussein's takeover of Kuwait the cause of the Persian Gulf War or merely a symptom of a more basic problem? When a fan belt breaks in a car, is that because the belt was old (a problem) or is it because the pulley is out of alignment (another kind of problem) and the belt broke under stress (a symptom.) When we solve symptoms rather than problems, the symptom will recur. If the belt broke because the pulley was out of alignment, changing the belt will simply result in another worn belt.

In order to help identify root problems, it is helpful to set out the criteria for a successful solution—to identify what will make for a good decision by clarifying the goal. Quality decisions are more likely to be made if the key factors in the situation are clearly identified as well. For example, in the Persian Gulf, what were the key personality, cultural, economic, and religious factors which existed before the decision to wage war?

Stating Assumptions

Decisions made today become actions in the future. So before any decision is made, a decision maker needs to clarify his or her assumptions about what the future will be like. Before George Bush could decide to enter the war with Iraq, he and his advisors needed to make a variety of assumptions about the future. Probably their assumptions included: the U.S. will remain dependent on oil for a significant time in the future, the U.S. will win the war if we enter it, Saddam Hussein will not leave Kuwait without a war, allies will help fight in and pay for a war, a stable Mideast is possible if Saddam Hussein is removed from power, a stable Mideast is not possible if Saddam Hussein is not removed from power.

Had they believed in a different set of assumptions, the decisions would most likely have been different. For example, what if their assumptions had been: alternative power sources and conservation will significantly reduce our reliance on oil in the next fifteen years; we will suffer many casualties if we enter a war, the cost of the war will result in sharply increased taxes; a Mideast war will result in a worldwide crisis.

Generating Alternatives

Given a certain problem and a set of assumptions about the future, typically many alternative solutions are possible. The very best decision makers give this step in the process special attention. Poor decision makers are quick to choose an alternative and commit to it, frequently relying on what has worked in the past. Decision makers willing to take risks and to consider a wide variety of alternatives are most likely to uncover creative solutions.

Generating a variety of creative alternatives is very difficult for many people because they self-judge and rule out ideas as unacceptable before they've even given the ideas a chance to develop. Several techniques have been developed to assist decision makers with the alternative-generation process.

Relaxation techniques help quiet the inner voices that judge ideas prematurely. In brainstorming, members of a group can bounce ideas off one another, add to what others said, and investigate ideas more fully. Writing lists of ideas with the "other" hand, the one not usually used, will frequently release more creative alternatives. Forced comparison is a techniques in which two or more lists of adjectives and nouns are placed side by side so that new alternatives are considered. Forced comparison was used to generate new toothpaste ideas. For generations, toothpaste was white. Now it comes striped, blue, green, or with sparkles.

Evaluating Alternatives and Choosing a Solution

Once a set of possible alternatives has been generated, the set is evaluated. Since nearly every alternative is likely to have both costs and benefits, choosing is difficult. Choosing an alternative may be rational or intuitive, but in either case it is sure to include social and political elements. Since many people may be involved in solving an organizational problem, the social and political elements of the alternatives can be very important.

One alternative to consider almost automatically is "doing nothing" or making no change. Change is not always good, even when problems exist with the current way of doing things. Serious consideration of creative alternatives may result in the thoughtful choice of leaving things as they are.

Implementing the Decision

The choice must become action. Many students of management are criticized when they begin their careers because, although they have developed skill at the previous steps in the decision-making process, they have not developed much skill at putting ideas into action. Implementation requires securing resources and gaining support for the decision. At 3M, researchers who develop product ideas may become the product's champion and present a complete implementation plan to top management. If they can convince the top decision makers that their plan is strong, the company will devote all the necessary capital and human resources to support the plan. In order to garner support and resources, political and human relations skills are required. Because very few plans are without cost, implementation requires a manager to reduce the negative consequences of the decision. Managers who fail to develop implementation skills make organizational enemies.

Monitoring the Results

Once a decision has become action, the results of the action must be monitored. The process of monitoring results is called controlling and will be discussed fully in chapter 19. Observing the consequences, intended and unintended, of a particular decision, is how managers learn what works best. The control or monitoring step becomes part of step one, analyzing the environment. Thus, the decision-making process is a continual one. Each decision leads to action, which results in the need for additional decision making.

BARRIERS TO CREATIVE PROBLEM SOLVING

Not all the decisions managers make are good ones. In fact, making effective decisions is so difficult that many managers avoid decision making whenever possible. Several barriers are likely to interfere with the rational decision-making process described above.

Avoiding Responsibility

Managers are held accountable for the quality of their decisions. Being responsible is difficult, so some managers try to avoid responsibility by avoiding decision making. Obviously, such behavior works only in the short run. In the longer run, managers who avoid decision making become pawns in others' games. The expression, "Not making a decision is merely your decision to let others control you" turns out to be true, frequently to the detriment of the organization. As Winston Churchill said, "Responsibility is the price of greatness."

Lack of Information

A common barrier to effective decision making is insufficient information. Lack of information can be the result of several conditions. Sometimes information is available, but it is not very accurate. Details on the lives of movie stars are available in any number of publications. However, the quality of the information may be questionable. Other times, excellent quality information would be available if enough time were devoted to getting it. Pharmaceutical companies must provide the Food and Drug Administration with reliable information on drug effectiveness, side effects, toxicity, purity, and so on. The information can take many years and hundreds of millions of dollars to obtain. The various levels of informational availability are called "states of nature." Managers must make decisions under these different conditions or states.

CONDITIONS OF CERTAINTY

When information is readily available, the decision maker has plenty of time to access it, and the outcomes of decision alternatives are known, the decision is being made under conditions of certainty. Needless to say, managers rarely have the good fortune to make decisions under such conditions.

CONDITIONS OF RISK

In a risk environment, the specific outcomes are not certain, but at least the probabilities of the possible outcomes are known. Probabilities are usually expressed as a percentage. For example, there is a 30 percent chance of interest rates falling by midsummer. Most managerial decisions are made under conditions of risk.

CONDITIONS OF UNCERTAINTY

Decisions made under conditions of uncertainty exist whenever the probability of potential outcomes is unknown. Perhaps even some of the alternatives are unknown. In rapidly changing business environments, uncertainty is often the rule. In such situations, the manager might try to reduce the uncertainty by basing the ultimate decision on past experience, hunches, intuition, or creativity.

Lack of Time

The steps in the rational decision-making process can be time consuming. In a crisis situation, managers do not have time. The more rapidly a decision must be made, the more important past experience is. Inexperienced managers are more likely to make poor quality decisions "under fire." The decision-making process can be categorized into three broad categories, each taking more time.

INTUITIVE DECISIONS

Intuition is problem solving that occurs without much conscious control. In some ways, it is the opposite of analysis. Rather than focusing on detailed information, intuitive problem solving seeks patterns in the whole. With intuition, the answer seems to "appear" in complete form. Frequently, an intuitive decision arises after the decision maker has given some careful attention to the problem and then has let the situation go from conscious attention. Thomas Edison said he would take an afternoon nap and awake with the answer to the problem he had worked on that morning. As researchers learn more about how the brain works, they gain confidence in the correctness of intuition.

JUDGMENTAL DECISIONS

Judgmental decisions are made on the basis of past experience. If, in the past, a manager successfully met a production deadline by relying on overtime, that manager is likely to decide overtime is the way to meet future deadlines. Judgment is the basis for the majority of daily managerial decisions. It is fast, inexpensive, and based on a readily available source of knowledge. There are problems with relying on judgment, though. Once a manager gets into a habit of responding in a particular way, he or she may fail to notice that the problem has changed slightly and that a more creative response is called for. Judgment also fails when the problem is complex or unusual. The more inexperienced the manager, the more likely poor decisions will result.

RATIONAL DECISIONS

Rational decision making is based on a linear process. The goal of the rational decision-making process is to reduce the amount of emotion in the choice made and to increase the objectivity with which the problem and its alternative solutions are considered. Although this process encourages the most careful consideration of the issues and alternatives, studies show the process is rarely followed, partly because it is so time consuming and partly because judgment, intuition, and emotion are important elements of decision making. Computer information systems have automated some parts of decision making, adding significant rationality to some types of decision situations.

Personal Values

Everyone, whether making individual decisions or decisions involving organizational resources, brings personal values and biases into the decision-making process. The degree to which a decision maker values profit over quality or certainty over risk affects the decision. Each individual looks at the world through his or her own experiences and perceptual filters. These individual biases color all the thinking and decision making a person does. The Ford Motor Company provides an excellent example of how individual values and perception affect major corporate decisions. In 1948, Ernest Breech, then President of Ford, went to Germany to decide if the Volkswagen factory was worth taking over as a contribution to war reparations. The factory's sole product was the Bug. Based on his experience in the auto industry and his personal taste for large cars, his verdict was: "The car is not worth a damn." Instead, Ford proceeded with the design and manufacture of a car "perfectly geared to American taste,"—the Edsel. Edsel sales were dismal, the car went out of production almost immediately, and the American public began buying smaller, plainer cars wherever they could find them. Breech built a car that pleased his taste, but he failed to identify the changes occurring in the tastes of the American buyer. By 1990, the Volkswagen Bug, still under production, had sold over twenty million units, the highest sales for any automobile ever.

SUPPORT FOR DECISION MAKERS

Organizations can, in a variety of situations, provide structural support to make decision making easier and more effective. The more inexperienced an organization's managers are, the more important such structural support is.

Programmed Decisions

A large number of problems are repetitive and well structured. In such instances, resources are wasted if each manager faced with the same problem analyzes the alternatives to find the best possible decision. When situations are repetitive and routine, programmed decisions can be institutionalized in the form of procedures, rules, and policies. For example, a store manager may be faced several times per day with customers who wish to return or exchange items. Rather than carefully analyzing the merits of each case, the manager simply applies the company policy. In many cases, programmed decision making is the result of precedent—managers simply do what they and others have done before. In other cases, top managers carefully and rationally consider alternatives and the consequences of them, and then develop organizationwide policies or procedures which managers must follow. Programmed decision making not only reduces the time any manager must spend on decision making, but also reduces personal responsibility and increases organizational consistency.

The more unstructured and nonrepetitive a problem is, the more a nonprogrammed decision is called for. For novel problems, such as the decision to make a subcomponent or buy it, a custom-made decision is essential. However, as organizations take more of a market or customer orientation, more nonprogrammed decisions are required on a daily basis. Organizations must choose between the efficiency of a programmed decision, and the effectiveness of nonprogrammed decisions.

Group Problem Solving

Another type of structural support an organization can use to assist decision makers is to encourage group problem solving. Individual and group decision-making processes each have their own strengths. When a manager lacks experience or information, group decision making is especially helpful. Group decisions have several specific advantages over individual decisions.

MORE COMPLETE INFORMATION

Because each of the members of a group brings his or her own information and values, the total group will have greater diversity of experience and perspective. As a result, the final decision will be based on a broader information base.

MORE ALTERNATIVES

Perhaps the most important contribution to creative problem solving is the generation of alternatives. When a group includes members with widely divergent backgrounds, expectations, or experience, it is more likely to generate a wide variety of alternatives.

GREATER ACCEPTANCE

If the people who will be affected by a decision, or who must implement it, are part of the decision-making process, they will be much more likely to accept the decision and encourage others to accept it. Group members who helped develop a solution are usually reluctant to undermine it. A decision that has input from more people is more likely to reflect the values and expectations of more people.

INCREASED LEGITIMACY

Participative decision making is valued in a democratic country. The more widely representative the group members are of the larger organizational community, the more legitimate the group's decision will seem.

DISPERSED RESPONSIBILITY

Some researchers claim that an advantage of group decision making is ambiguous responsibility. Since group members share responsibility, no one person is responsible for the final outcome. In most situations, shared responsibility is a powerful support mechanism for decision makers.

DISADVANTAGES OF GROUP DECISION MAKING

In certain situations, individual problem solving is a better choice. Some disadvantages of group decision making may interfere with the quality of a group's solution. Typically, group decision making takes much more time. The coordination process must be added to the decision-making process. Schedules must be coordinated, knowledge and information shared, assumptions discussed, and alternatives generated by a number of people.

As alternatives and solutions are discussed, a lack of consensus may arise, which can lead to infighting and bitterness. Sometimes the bitterness is more damaging to organizational effectiveness than the original problem.

Status and politics may influence the final decision, as lower-status members try to placate or impress higher-status members.

Because the responsibility for the final decision is shared by all the group members, no one can be held personally to blame. While this observation can encourage group members to try more creative solutions, it also means that poor decisions can "slip by" without thoughtful analysis of what went wrong.

Reward Structures

Managers are most likely to do what they are rewarded for doing. If the organization says it supports risk taking and environmental sensitivity and then rewards short-term profitability and punishes mistakes, managers will very soon adapt to what is rewarded.

**Quantitative
Methods**

Very complex problems, especially those that are largely quantifiable, may be best analyzed using a math-based model. Rate of return on investment and inventory turnover are examples of frequently used quantitative methods that help decision makers. When the problem is more complex, more complex mathematical analysis can be employed. Some of the most frequently used quantitative models include the payoff matrix, the decision tree, linear programming, and queuing theory. Most students of management learn about these tools in a course in quantitative methods.

CONTINGENCY PLANNING

Effective decision makers give consideration to what they will do if the solution they have chosen does not meet their expectations. Some planning experts refer to this as Plan B. Suppose an organization has a goal of selling one hundred units more this quarter, and the plan is to increase newspaper advertising to accomplish this goal. Newspaper advertising is Plan A. Now suppose that after two months, sales have not changed. An effective decision maker has already considered this possibility. Rather than giving up the goal of increasing sales, the manager switches to Plan B, the backup solution. Newspaper advertising is reduced to previous levels, and a radio advertising campaign is initiated. This process is called contingency planning. Backup planning is important because decisions are based on assumptions about the future. Those assumptions can be wrong. In the chapters on planning that follow this one, this factor in decision making will be addressed further.

As the essential managerial function, high-quality decision making is crucial to managerial and organizational success. Because both the internal and external environments of organizations are changing, creative solutions to problems are called for. Knowing and following the decision-making process—environmental analysis, problem recognition, problem identification, stating assumptions, generating alternatives, evaluating alternatives in search of a solution, implementing the decision, and monitoring the results—can improve the quality of a manager's decisions.

Special focus on generating many alternatives and on thinking about the social and political effects of implementation will help all managers, especially those with limited experience in making decisions that effect others. Because managers may wish to avoid the responsibility which goes along with decision making, they may find group decision making more comfortable as well as more effective. In the chapters that follow, the critical role effective decision making plays in organizational management will become obvious.

Selected Readings

Adams, J. L. 1979. *Conceptual Blockbusting: A Guide to Better Ideas*, 2nd ed. New York: Norton.

Agor, Weston H. 1986. "The Logic of Intuition: How Top Executives Make Important Decisions." *Organizational Dynamics* 14: 5–18.

Cowan, David A. 1986. "Developing a Process Model of Problem Recognition." *Academy of Management Review* 11: 763–776.

Georgoff, D. M., and R. G. Murdick. 1986. "Manager's Guide to Forecasting." *Harvard Business Review* 65: 112–120.

Grassman, W. K. 1988. "Finding the Right Number of Servers in Real-World Systems." *Interfaces* March/April: 94–104.

Kaplan, Robert E. 1985. *Whatever It Takes: Decision Makers at Work*. Englewood Cliffs, NJ: Prentice Hall.

Maier, Norman R. F. 1963. *Problem-Solving Discussions and Conferences: Leadership Methods and Skills*. New York: McGraw-Hill.

Meyer, Alan D. 1984. "Mingling Decision-Making Metaphors." *Academy of Management Review* 9: 6–17.

Simon, Herbert A. 1977. *The New Science of Management Decision*. Englewood Cliffs, NJ: Prentice Hall.

Simon, Herbert A. 1983. *Reason in Human Affairs*. Stanford, CA: Stanford University Press.

Soelberg, P. O. 1967. "Unprogrammed Decision Making." *Industrial Management Review* 6: 577–587.

Tylecote, Andrew. 1987. "Time Horizons of Management Decisions: Causes and Effects." *Journal of Economic Studies* 14: 51–64.

7

The Planning Process

*O*n *the book jacket of novelist Richard Bach's book,* One, *is the following: "I gave my life to become the person I am at this moment. Was it worth it?" Planning allows individuals and organizations to determine in advance what they want to become and thus to answer more certainly that the cost was worth it.*

Regardless of the level of management, effective planning is the key to efficient accomplishment of objectives. Plans are like road maps. They do not assure successful arrival at the destination, but they most certainly reduce the time spent traveling down wrong roads. Organizational planning provides direction, reduces the overall impact of both internal and external change, and increases productivity.

Planning is a proactive event—it allows an organization to prepare for change, rather than merely react to it. Planning is an essential part of effective action.

PLANNING DEFINED

Planning is the process of deciding in advance what to accomplish and how to accomplish it. There are several important elements in this definition. First, planning is a process. That means it is ongoing and part of the total process of managing. It is dynamic. Second, planning is future directed. Planning decisions, while made in the present, are concerned with deciding the future, in advance. Finally, planning establishes not only the ends, or what the organization hopes to accomplish, but also the means, or how the ends will be met.

THE PURPOSE OF PLANNING

Organizations are effective because of the coordinated effort of people working together. Plans provide a shared understanding of the direction the organization wants to go. As a result, plans are helpful coordination tools. They reduce overlap and wasteful activities.

Planning forces managers to look ahead and anticipate the changes they are likely to encounter. As discussed in the chapter on decision making, planning requires that assumptions about the future be clarified.

Planning establishes objectives or standards which, when compared with actual performance, facilitate control. When an organization is unclear on what it hopes to achieve, it has no sense of how well it is doing. Planning is an integral part of controlling.

Finally, according to a 1984 review in *Journal of Management* by Shrader, Taylor, and Dalton, most studies show that managers who plan outperform nonplanners on traditional financial measures, such as profits. So for many reasons, planning is an important managerial activity.

THE PLANNING PROCESS

Planning begins with an understanding of the organizational mission. From the mission statement, specific objectives or goals can be established. Then tactical or operational plans can be developed to accomplish the objectives.

Mission Statements

A mission is a continuing purpose or reason for being. A mission statement is a broadly stated definition of the basic purpose and scope of the organization. Another way of stating it is that the mission statement tells the unique reason for the organization's existence. For example, United Parcel Service (UPS) "runs the tightest ship in the shipping business." Toys "R" Us Inc. "sells toys as if Christmas were always around the corner." Merck's mission is to be the "untouchable number one pharmaceutical company in the world."

A mission provides an organization with direction over time. Although organizations may change their strategy for reaching their missions, rarely do they change their purpose for being. When they do, the change is almost always to a broader statement. Shell has changed from being in the oil business to being in the energy business. For decades, the March of Dimes had as its mission the eradication of polio. The organization was so successful that for a while it had no direction, and donations to the nonprofit fund were way down. Now, the organization's purpose or mission is to fight birth defects, a broader mission which will most likely provide direction for a very long time.

Objectives

Once an organization has a mission, specific goals or objectives can be established. Objectives are desired end results. Typically, top management sets corporate objectives, which may be something like increase market share by 2 percent per year, improve worker productivity by 2 percent per year, and introduce at least one new product per year. Then middle management sets objectives for each unit. Their goal is to make unit objectives support or be congruent with corporate objectives. For example, as part of the corporate objective to increase market share by 2 percent per year, the sales department may have objectives like increase sales force by three people this year and provide at least three training workshops for all sales personnel this year. Lower-level or supervisory managers will then establish more specific objectives for each of their specific areas of responsibility. For example, the personnel manager in the sales unit may have objectives like advertise for sales personnel in four major newspapers by March, recruit on at least twelve college campuses by April, arrange candidate interviews with sales manager by June.

CHARACTERISTICS OF OBJECTIVES

Mission, objective, and plan can all be informal—something generally agreed to in conversation among organizational members. However, in order to serve as clear guidelines for coordinating organizational activity, a more formal approach to the planning process is important. Objectives are most effective when they meet the following qualifications.

Clearly Written. Actually stating objectives in writing appears to have powerful impact on the accomplishment of the objectives. On a personal level, Harvard Business School graduates, class of 1980, were asked a series of questions when they graduated. One of the questions was: "Do you have a list of written goals?" Ten years later, those graduates who answered "yes" to that question had a financial net worth many times that of the graduates who answered "no." In addition, the graduates with a list of written objectives perceived themselves to be much happier and more satisfied with their lives. Evidence on organizational effectiveness mirrors these findings. Writing objectives down and leaving them where they can be referred to increases the likelihood of their being reached.

Measurable. Objectives are more effective when those involved can tell if the objective has been reached. "Increase sales by 10 percent" is a clearer objective than "increase sales." "Reduce customer complaints to no more than six per one million dollars in sales" is a more effective goal or objective than "improve customer relations."

Time-Specific. Setting a time frame for achieving an objective helps get things moving. When people have a great deal to accomplish, they tend to work on those projects with a deadline. Making objectives time-specific makes them more real and immediate. "Hire replacement accountant by June 15" is a clearer goal than "hire an accountant to replace Bob."

Challenging but Attainable. Objectives can be motivating or demotivating. They are most likely to be motivating when they are difficult enough to provide a challenge, yet not so difficult that they are unattainable. When an objective is challenging, the achiever of the objective feels successful. When an objective is too easy, it provides no stimulation or motivation. On the other hand, when the objective is impossible, the result is most likely to be a complete lack of effort.

REAL VERSUS STATED OBJECTIVES

Sometimes, the objectives an organization claims to strive for are not the objectives organizational members are rewarded for achieving. For example, many companies tell potential customers that they have a customer service orientation. At the same time, employees have their pay docked if more than 2 percent of items are returned. If the stated objective is quality while employees are rewarded for producing quantity, real objectives do not match stated objectives.

CONSISTENCY

When stated objectives match real objectives, greater progress will of course be made in achieving them. The same is true for objectives that consistently support each other from the top level to the bottom level of the organization. Every unit produced on the assembly line ideally contributes to the organization's mission. Every report written or piece of paper filed should help the organization meets its objectives. In order to accomplish this ideal state, two things need to happen. First, the mission and organizational objectives must be set and clearly communicated by top management. And second, every manager down the hierarchy must consider whether the work being done in his or her unit effectively and efficiently assists in progress toward the mission.

Coordination across functional levels is also important. For example, the goals of the production department will need to be coordinated. If the sales department is expecting 10 percent more product, then the production department will need to produce 10 percent more.

MULTIPLE OBJECTIVES

Even after the organization and its managers have clarified the objectives and made certain they mesh well and contribute to the organizational mission, employees might have trouble making consistent progress toward their accomplishment. Frequently, more objectives exist than can be reasonably handled by the available human and material resources. So it becomes necessary not only to make certain objectives are consistent across managerial and functional levels, but to prioritize them as well. Which is the most important goal for this unit? Which is the least important, to be tackled only if time and resources are available?

QUANTIFIABLE VERSUS NONQUANTIFIABLE OBJECTIVES

One of the suggested characteristics of effective objectives is measurability. The problem is some of the most important components of organizational effectiveness are not necessarily quantifiable. How might an organization tell if it has enlarged its goodwill this year? Are good community relations measured by the number of presentations given by the CEO?

In every organization, some objectives will be easily quantifiable and some will not be. What frequently happens is that the most measurable objectives receive the most attention, whether or not they are the most important objectives. For example, in a university, it is relatively easy to measure the number of articles a professor writes and the dollars of grants a department receives. It is very difficult to determine what constitutes excellent teaching and even more difficult to measure it.

Plans

A plan states the means a person or an organization will use to reach the objectives. It is a framework that details the methods and tasks involved in achieving the goal. There are a variety of taxonomies for categorizing plans—by breadth, time frame, specificity, and management level. A particularly helpful way to consider the different types of plans is to separate them into strategic plans, which are very broad, and tactical or operational plans, which are more specific.

STRATEGIC PLANS

Strategic plans are the broadest and are usually developed by top management with help from staff strategists. Essentially, they attempt to answer the questions "What business are we in?" and "How shall we compete in our industry?" As an example of a strategy, Lucky Supermarkets have chosen to compete in the full-service grocery store industry on the basis of everyday low price. The chain does not run special sales, but rather advertises overall low prices.

OPERATIONAL PLANS

Operational plans set out the tactics or specific steps the organization will use to follow its strategic plan. Operational plans are also called action plans, because they identify certain actions that will be taken by certain people within a stated time frame. Action plans take good ideas and make them more concrete and specific. They set out the implementation steps. There are two types of operational plans—single-use plans and standing plans.

Single-Use Plans. As the name implies, single-use plans are developed when a particular activity is not likely to be repeated. The construction of a new factory, the development of a new product, or the training of a new employee are all activities for which a single-use plan might be developed. Budgets also fall under this category. Although it may be unusual to think of them this way, budgets are plans that specify allocations of financial resources required to support specific activities within a given period. Schedules are single-use plans that specify allocations of human resources. Schedules are usually developed by the lowest-level managers, and are likely to cover very short periods of time—perhaps a week, perhaps a day.

Standing Plans. Many activities recur repeatedly in organizations. In such cases, a plan can be developed that can be used over and over. Standing plans conserve time and energy, allowing managers to focus on the non-recurring events. The three types of standing plans are policies, procedures, and rules.

1. *Policy* is a standing plan which provides a general guideline for decision making. Policies set boundaries or limits within which decisions can be made. For example, "Checks may be cashed up to a limit of three hundred dollars" allows an employee to use judgment in deciding whether or not to cash a particular forty dollar check, and sets the boundary at which the employee must decide not to accept any check. Policies reduce the need for close supervision. They also serve to communicate organizational values. Policies that leave a great deal of decision making leeway to the employee communicate greater trust and desire for employee participation. Policies that allow very little room for individual discretion in decision making communicate lower trust. They reduce both personal and organizational flexibility.

2. *Procedures* (sometimes called standard operating procedures) are standing plans which govern specific actions in specific situations. Usually procedures specify step-by-step actions. Procedures are especially useful for training new employees and helping them fit into an organization rapidly. Most retail stores have a procedure for accepting payment by check. An example might be: (1) check to see that the amount of the check matches the amount of the receipt, (2) verify the signature with the driver's license

signature, (3) write the driver's license number on the front of the check, and (4) initial by the license number.

3. *Rules* are the most explicit form of standing plan. They require that a certain action be taken or be avoided. For example, "No smoking" is a rule forbidding an action. "Eye protection must be worn in this area" is a rule requiring an action. Rules eliminate the need for decision making entirely. Usually rules carry with them a written or unwritten sanction for failure to obey.

Policies, procedures, and rules are helpful tools for coordinating and directing the activities of organizational members.

Contingency Planning	Environmental uncertainty makes it difficult to project critical factors in the future. As was pointed out in chapter 6, under these conditions, managers will try to develop contingency plans. Contingency planning involves identifying alternative courses of action in advance, thus reducing crises. Contingency planning is based on a series of evaluations. (1) In the development of a plan, managers can identify action points where the commitment of additional resources will be required. (2) At each action point, before going on with the commitment, a new analysis of possible environmental events is made, and the probability of each event occurring is estimated. For example, there may be a 60 percent probability that interest rates will fall by more than 2 percent, a 30 percent probability that interest rates will remain about the same, and a 10 percent probability that interest rates will actually increase by more than 1 percent. A contingency plan is developed for each event having high probability. (3) While the next step of the project is underway, environmental conditions are monitored. (4) If a decision is made that an event is likely to occur, implementation of the appropriate contingency plan can begin. In the example, if interest rates do indeed appear to be dropping more than 2 percent, the company might want to consider borrowing development money, rather than selling stock to raise money. (5) Action points are continually checked for further contingency events.

BARRIERS TO EFFECTIVE PLANNING AND OVERCOMING THEM

The evidence that thoughtful planning is essential to efficient goal attainment is conclusive. In spite of that, individuals and organizations often put planning at the end of their list of important things to do. When that happens, powerful barriers must be present. Certainly, planning is difficult, since it requires a search for data, a rigorous analysis of those data, and concentrated mental effort. Many otherwise successful managers find this effort just too much for them. But other barriers are often present as well.

Forecasting Problems

Although plans are made today, they are made based on forecasts (or educated guesses) about what will happen in the future. As chapters 3 and 4 pointed out, both internal and external changes are happening so fast that ability to forecast the future accurately is diminished. When projections about the future are inaccurate, plans made on those projections are certain to be poor ones. After several aborted attempts at planning, some managers would rather quit trying and just take each day as it comes.

However, more and more industries are developing industry boards or councils. These councils are supported by membership fees. One of the primary tasks of industry councils is to collect and interpret data that might have an impact on the future of the industry. Industry councils might also be charged with establishing standards for the industry and with lobbying efforts. The hoped-for result of these tasks is reducing unanticipated environmental change, thus improving forecasting quality.

Time Consuming

Planning requires thoughtful analysis, not only of external information, but of the strengths and weaknesses of the firm and of organizational and personal values. As a result, it is time consuming. Some organizations are so involved in day-to-day crises, they cannot imagine taking time out for an activity that has no immediate result. Because effective plans require organizationwide coordination, committee work is almost always involved, and many managers have a bias against committee work.

However, time spent planning typically reduces time spent in crisis. Crisis management is stressful, exhausting, and inefficient. Planning, although mentally difficult, tends to be rejuvenating and stress-reducing because it puts things in perspective and reestablishes priorities.

Reduces Flexibility

Once a plan has been established, and resources have been committed to it, alternative plans must be abandoned. It is true that the more an organization or individual sets objectives and establishes plans, the less flexibility there is to seek other goals. The reality, though, is that there are not time and resources enough to do all things. With a mission, objectives, and plans, the chances of reaching those objectives go way up. With no plan and flexible objectives, the chances of accomplishing anything, much less everything, are much lower. As John-Roger and Peter McWilliam say in *Life 101*, "you can have anything you want, you just can't have everything you want."

However, reduced flexibility need not mean inflexibility. Periodic reviews of existing plans may be a necessary aid in minimizing a tendency toward inflexibility. Even strategic planning, typically long range, is not permanent. In February 1989, Sears, Roebuck & Company changed its entire corporate strategy, expanding its product line and reducing its prices.

Fear

Fear of failure and fear of change may be significant barriers to effective planning. Planning acknowledges the presence of goals. Managers who are afraid they and their subordinates will be unable to meet the goals may resist the planning process entirely.

Although not always, the planning process may result in significant organizational change. As chapter 24 addresses more fully, many people are afraid of change. They fear they will not be able to learn new methods or reach new objectives. Fear of change can result in resistance to planning.

Top management commitment, additional training, and involvement of a broad base of employees in the planning process will help reduce fear barriers to planning.

Getting there is easier if you know where "there" is. The planning process—establishing organizational mission, objectives, and plans—is critical to organizational effectiveness and efficiency.

In spite of significant barriers, good managers work at being good planners. Lower-level managers are responsible for operational plans with a short planning horizon, middle managers are responsible for coordinating operational plans among levels and functional areas, and top management takes a long-range view, focusing on organizational mission and strategy.

Selected Readings

Allaire, Yvan, and Mihaela Firsirotu. 1988. "Coping with Strategic Uncertainty." *Sloan Management Review* 30: 7–15.

Armstrong, J. Scott. 1985. *Long-Range Forecasting: From Crystal Ball to Computer*. New York: Wiley.

Drucker, Peter. 1954. *The Practice of Management*. New York: Harper & Row, for an introduction to managing by objectives.

Drucker, Peter. 1980. *Managing in Turbulent Times*. New York: Harper & Row, for a thoughtful discussion of planning in an uncertain environment.

Linsay, W. M., and L.W. Rue. 1980. "Impact of the Organization Environment on the Long-Range Planning Process: A Contingency View." *Academy of Management Journal* 23: 385–404.

Mento, Anthony J., R. P. Steel, and R. J. Karren. 1987. "A Meta-Analytic Study of the Effects of Goal Setting on Task Performance: 1966–1984." *Organizational Behavior and Human Decision Processes* Feb: 52–83.

Morrisey, George. 1988. "Who Needs a Mission Statement? You Do." *Training and Development Journal* 42: 50–52.

Pearce, John, and Fred David. 1987. "Corporate Mission Statements: The Bottom Line." *Academy of Management Executive* May: 109–115.

Rhyne, Lawrence. 1987. "Contrasting Planning Systems in High, Medium, and Low Performance Companies." *Journal of Management Studies* July: 363–385.

Toffler, Alvin. 1990. *Power Shift*. New York: Bantam Books.

8

Strategic Planning: Planning Long Range

In Lewis Carroll's Alice in Wonderland, *the Cheshire Cat says to Alice, "If you don't know where you're going, then any road will take you there." This chapter discusses how an organization decides where it is going. The next chapter discusses how an organization determines which road to take to get there.*

Strategic planning is planning for the long run. Organizations occasionally change their strategy, but rarely. As a result, deciding where the organization is going is very important, and requires very careful consideration. Errors in strategic planning are frequently fatal to the organization.

In the last chapter, the basic planning process indicated that good planning starts with an organizational mission statement. The first task of strategic planning is establishing the mission statement. The next task in strategic planning is to identify the overall approach the organization will use to further its mission. Several tools have been developed to help managers think clearly about setting the organization's strategic direction. This chapter discusses those tools.

STRATEGIC PLANNING DEFINED

Strategic planning consists of those activities leading to the definition of the organization's mission, the setting of objectives, and the development of strategies that enable it to function successfully in its environment. Strategic planning is different from other types of organizational planning. According to management scholars John Pearce and R. B. Robinson, strategic planning:

1. Involves decisions made by top management;

2. Involves ultimate allocation of large amounts of resources, such as money, labor, or physical capacity;

3. Has significant long-term impact;

4. Focuses on the organization's interaction with the external environment.

In 1978, Charles Hofer and Dan Schendel reviewed the strategy literature and identified an integrated definition of strategic planning that considers four components.

1. The need to match products or markets with geographic territories (the scope of the organization);

2. The need to deploy a large quantity and variety of resources, both human and material;

3. The need to recognize and seize competitive advantages;

4. The need to convince a complex variety of functional divisions that departmental cooperation is better for overall organizational performance than isolated departmental activity.

LEVELS OF STRATEGY

Large conglomerates such as General Electric, which manufactures aircraft engines and light bulbs and owns the NBC television network, or Eastman Kodak, with film, pharmaceutical, chemical, battery, and other divisions, are in a variety of businesses. As a result, they need several levels of strategy—corporate, business unit, and functional levels.

Corporate-Level Strategy

Corporate-level strategy seeks to provide an overall focus for the variety of businesses the corporation owns. This strategy seeks to answer the question: "In what set of businesses should we be?" It also determines the roles that each business in the organization will play. Based on corporate-level strategy, an organization will decide which additional businesses to acquire and which businesses to sell off. When Sears, Roebuck & Company decided to pursue a strategy of price leadership, it made the decision to divest the Coldwell Banker Realty Group, because that business unit no longer fit Sears's strategy.

Business-Level Strategy

Each business unit in a multibusiness corporation needs its own strategy. At this level, strategic planning attempts to answer the question "How should we compete in each of our businesses?" Within the General Motors Corporation, for example, are divisional business units—Chevrolet, Cadillac, Oldsmobile—each of which has its own unique strategy. Cadillac focuses on the top end of the customers for automobiles, offering relatively expensive models. The Chevrolet division takes a high-volume, lower-price strategy to marketing its models.

When the business units owned by one corporation are very different from one another, different business-level strategies for each are especially important.

A multibusiness corporation can manage its strategic business units like a portfolio of stock and bond investments. Although some business units will make money, and some will instead require investment of capital, overall the multibusiness corporation will be profitable. For example, the year that McNeill lost money on its Tylenol product, the parent company, Johnson & Johnson, was still profitable.

Functional-Level Strategy

Within each business is a variety of functional areas, sometimes called departments. These might include sales, production, personnel, research and development, and finance. Strategic planning at this level attempts to answer the question, "In our functional area, how do we support the business-level strategy?" Suppose the business-level strategy is to "market the product line worldwide." A supportive functional-level strategy for the research and development department, for example, might then be modifying the product line so that it can readily adapt to the variety of power voltages different countries use.

TECHNIQUES IN STRATEGIC PLANNING

A number of frameworks have been developed for helping managers think about the concept of strategy. In general, the frameworks assist managers in carefully assessing the external environment and internal capabilities of the organization.

Peter Lorange, strategic management scholar and consultant, says that any particular method of strategic management must answer four very simple questions which take into consideration both the planning and action components of the concept of strategy:

1. Where are we going?
2. How do we get there?
3. What's our blueprint for action?
4. How do we know if we are on track?

The BCG Matrix

The Boston Consulting Group (BCG) developed a model of strategy that emphasizes the internal mix or diversification of business units in a multi-business organization. The objective of the BCG matrix is to help managers decide the best use of internal resources. The matrix is based on three aspects of a particular business unit—its sales, the growth of its market, and whether it absorbs or produces cash in its operations. The classification of business units within the matrix leads to four strategic types—stars, cash cows, question marks, and dogs. Each type describes a business in a different stage of development, each with unique implications for overall corporate strategy.

STARS

A business in the "star" category has both high market growth rate and a relatively large share of the market. Typically, stars are businesses with a high potential for growth and profits. However, because they are growing rapidly, they require substantial, continual investment. An example of a star might be a genetics engineering company or a developer/producer of high-definition televisions.

CASH COWS

A cash cow is a business with a relatively high market share in a mature, slow-growth industry. Because significant investment in facilities or advertising is no longer required, cash cows produce surplus cash. The multibusiness corporation can "milk" this type of strategic unit to provide investment funds for stars. An example of a cash cow would be Mars Candy Company's Snickers and Mars bars, or Kimberly-Clark's Kleenex products.

QUESTION MARKS

A question mark is the most problematic for managers formulating a business plan. Question mark businesses have a relatively small market share in a rapidly growing industry. The rapid growth of the market may require heavy investment simply to maintain a low share of the market, even though that low share may yield low or even negative profits and cash flow. Increasing the market share would require still larger investments. However, the rapid growth of the market segment offers exciting opportunities if the proper business strategy and the investment to implement it can be found. Over the last ten years, the computer industry has seen some question mark businesses become shining stars, while others have become expensive losses.

DOGS

The dog holds a relatively low market share in a stagnant or, at best, a slowly growing market. Usually, dogs are a cash drain on the organization because they are unable to support themselves on the revenue they generate. Black and white television producers most likely find themselves in this category.

The "success sequence" in the BCG matrix involves investing excess cash from cash cows into promising question mark businesses to allow them to grow into stars. When the rate of market growth slows for the stars, they will become cash cows, generating cash to invest in the next generation. A company may not want to carry a dog. Its role in the strategic plan would be the deciding factor.

Porter's Strategic Forces

Management scholar Michael Porter has identified five forces that influence success in a particular business or industry. The corporate strategist analyzes these forces and develops a program for influencing or defending against them.

THREAT OF ENTRY

Certain factors influence how easily competitors will be able to enter a market and provide significant competition. Some of these factors include brand identification, capital requirements, access to distribution channels, government policy, and economies of scale. As an example, environmental impact laws and regulations may block entry of a new ski resort. An established resort can use lobbying to lower threat of competitors.

BARGAINING POWER OF CUSTOMERS

When customers are willing to see a product as undifferentiated, competition increases, and overall profitability decreases. In order to reduce competition, businesses can differentiate more and use advertising to encourage customers to value the differentiation. IBM-compatible computers have had a downward influence on the price of IBM computers.

BARGAINING POWER OF SUPPLIERS

If the number of suppliers is very small, suppliers can become a powerful influence on the purchasers' profitability. When Chrysler first brought out the Omni/Horizon models, Volkswagen supplied the engines. Many more of the new models were demanded than Volkswagen was willing to supply engines for. Chrysler lost potential sales. In professional sports, players' unions can exert a strong influence because there are few substitutes and the "product" is critical to the buyers' business.

SUBSTITUTE PRODUCTS

If the customer perceives that less expensive substitutes exist for a business's product, then profitability will decrease. An interesting example of substitute products effecting profitability is the impact of artificial sweeteners on the demand for sugar. In addition to artificial sweeteners, cane sugar has direct competition from beet sugar, corn syrup, and honey.

COMPETITOR RIVALRY

In some industries, competition among existing companies is especially fierce. Advertising slugfests, price wars, and increased warranties can effect profitability. The airline industry offers numerous examples of competitor rivalry resulting in price wars, frequent flyer programs, and even takeovers.

Porter's framework indicates that the greater the forces in an industry, the lower the expected profitability. In order to be successful in an industry with many new entrants, a large number of substitute products, few suppliers, savvy purchasers, and intense rivalry from competitors, a company must develop a strategy that takes these forces into account.

SWOT Analysis

SWOT is an acronym for Strengths and Weaknesses internal to the organization and Opportunities and Threats in the organization's external environment. A SWOT analysis helps strategists build a plan that emphasizes strengths and opportunities.

STRENGTHS

Strengths are sometimes referred to as distinctive competencies. They might include technology, patents, skills, resources, market position, and so forth, which gives the organization a competitive advantage in the marketplace. When Apple Computer was developing the Macintosh, the energy and excitement shared by the employees was a real strength. Typically, employees worked 12–14 hours per day.

WEAKNESSES

A weakness is an internal condition that can lead to poor organizational performance. Some typical weaknesses might include too much debt, old plant and equipment, focus on a single product, poor location, weak managerial skills, or poor product image. As an example, when an organization has had a strong, highly competent leader for several years, it may fail to develop managerial skills in others. When Wal-Mart's founder, Sam Walton, retires, the company may go through a period of vulnerability.

OPPORTUNITIES

An opportunity is a current or future condition in the environment which an organization could use to its advantage. For the medical industry, the aging of the population is an opportunity since older people typically require more medical care than younger people. Changes in the law can create new opportunities. When the federal income tax law was revised in 1986, the demand for vacation homes escalated because the mortgage interest on them was tax deductable. As environmental protection becomes more important to the public, developers of alternative energy sources have more opportunities. The twentieth Earth Day, and the environmental awareness it encouraged, suddenly increased the demand for diaper services. As these examples show, some opportunities can be predicted with high certainty; others cannot.

THREATS

A threat is a current or future environmental condition that may prove harmful to an organization. For example, as the number of children 16–20 decreased, fast food restaurants had to adapt to reduced labor supplies. Higher gas taxes may reduce the demand for recreational vehicles. Stricter government standards for exhaust emissions may threaten the profitability of auto makers.

By using SWOT analysis, organizations can obtain a clearer picture of their strategic position. However, in addition to making lists, the strategic planner will need to assign weights and probabilities and apply other evaluative measures to the factors identified. Not all opportunities are equally profitable and not all weaknesses are equally damaging.

STRATEGIC ALTERNATIVES

A variety of strategic alternatives are available to strategic planners. Based on the types of analyses discussed here, an organization will choose the alternative strategic "road" most likely to help it reach its mission and objectives.

Some of the most frequently followed strategic alternatives include the following.

Concentration When an organization follows a strategy of concentration, it operates within a single industry. Dr. Pepper produces only soft drinks, McDonald's operates only fast food restaurants, and Polaroid is exclusively in the instant picture business. The major advantages of concentration are clarity of objectives and a singular organizational focus. The danger with concentration, of course, is that any major threat to the industry is a major threat to the entire organization.

Vertical Integration

In a vertically integrated company, the organization expands backwards towards its sources of supply or forward to the end user. A cattle rancher might choose to raise corn and alfalfa. Stu Leonard's famous grocery store started as the vertical integration of a dairy farmer who opened his own dairy products store, then expanded to a produce store, and then expanded to a major supermarket. Simply Cotton, a chain of retail clothing stores, started as a wholesaler of imported cotton fabrics. The owners began arranging to have their fabrics made into clothing and then decided to retail the clothing themselves.

The big advantages of vertical integration are greater control of the distribution chain and greater control over end-product costs. The major disadvantages are the requirement of additional capital and increased complexity of management. Operating a dairy is nothing like operating a successful supermarket.

Diversification

Diversification is the opposite of concentration. The strategy is to enter a business different from the ones the organization is already involved in. Some organizations enter related fields. For example, Head, a manufacturer of snow skis, diversified into tennis rackets, and then into sports clothing. Tennis rackets and snow skis tend to be countercyclical, which smooths out the demand for the company's products. Other organizations choose to enter completely unrelated fields. For example, ITT, originally a telecommunications company, now owns Sheraton Hotels and Hartford Insurance, among other businesses. The advantage of dissimilar diversification is that a decline in one industry will not necessarily mean a decline for the corporation as a whole. The major disadvantage of diversification is that the management of the company becomes increasingly complex as the diversity of subunits increases. It is more difficult for diverse companies to answer the question "What business are we in?"

Cost Leadership

A cost leadership strategy means that the organization will be the lowest-price competitor in the industry. In order to accomplish this strategy, the company must focus on lowering costs. Construction of efficient facilities, tight cost and overhead control, minimal customer service, and low advertising costs are all important to organizations taking a cost leadership strategy. Typically, cost leadership is profitable only when the company holds a high percent of the total market. The advantage of this strategy is a large customer base. Briggs and Stratton, which holds 50 percent of the worldwide market for small gasoline engines, is an example of a company taking the cost leadership strategy.

Differentiation

An organization taking the differentiation strategy seeks to provide a unique product. The adoption of a differentiation strategy means that a high market share will be sacrificed in exchange for a high margin. Rather than taking cost leadership, which implies lowest price to the consumer, differentiation is taking price leadership, or highest price to the consumer. Mercedes has taken this strategy in its automobile division. Hoffman suitcases offer another example of differentiation strategy. Consumers will pay more to have the name, not only for the quality product, but for the status as well. The risk with this strategy is that, even though customers may recognize the superiority of the product, they may be unwilling to pay the high price.

Strategic planning consists of defining an organization's mission and developing the strategies that will enable it to function successfully in its environment. A number of important internal and external variables affect an organization's strategy.

An organization's strategy is chosen for the long run. Top management commits significant resources in an attempt to exploit the organization's strengths and minimize its weaknesses. In spite of that, strategies can and should change to take advantage of opportunites and threats in the environment.

Strategic planning has become increasingly important, especially because of the increasing complexity of the environment and the increasing size of business organizations. However strategy must become action. The next chapter discusses methods for implementing strategy in the short run.

Selected Readings

Haspeslagh, Philippe. 1982. "Portfolio Planning: Uses and Limits." *Harvard Business Review* 60: 58–73.

Jackson, Susan E. and Jane E. Dutton. 1988. "Discerning Threats and Opportunities." *Administrative Science Quarterly* Sept: 370–387.

Leontiades, James. 1986. "Going Global—Global Strategies vs. National Strategies." *Long Range Planning* Dec: 96–104.

Pearce, John and R. B. Robinson. 1985. *Strategic Management*, 2nd ed. Homewood, IL: Irwin.

Porter, Michael. 1980. *Competitive Strategy: Techniques for Analyzing Industries and Competitors*. New York: Free Press.

Thompson, A. A., Jr., and A. J. Strickland. 1987. *Strategic Management: Concepts and Cases*. Plano, TX: Business Publications.

Weigelt, Keith, and Ian MacMillan. 1988. "An Interactive Strategic Analysis Framework." *Strategic Management Journal* 9: 27–40.

Willis, Rod. 1987. "ServiceMaster: The Details Make the Whole Thing Work." *Management Review* Oct: 26–28.

9

Planning for Implementation—Planning Short Range

All organizations work within the constraints of limited time and limited resources. Somehow, managers must allocate time and resources to the varied tasks necessary to reach the organization's objectives. The planning required to do this is called tactical or operational planning. Its goal is to implement, or put into action, the strategic plans of the organization.

Strategic planning is the responsibility of top management. But all managers have operational planning responsibility. This chapter discusses in greater detail operational planning, and suggests some tools managers can use to assist them in planning for the day-to-day operations of the organization.

ANNUAL OBJECTIVES

Operational planning might be thought of as strategy implementation. It is the process of making daily progress toward organizational objectives. The first step in operational planning is setting annual objectives. Annual objectives identify precisely what must be accomplished each year in order to achieve the organization's strategic goals. If Merck's corporate objective is to remain the untouchable leader in pharmaceuticals, then the sales department might have an annual objective of making contact with an additional 10 percent of all physicians. Annual objectives provide managers with specific targets for the coming year's performance. They clarify managers' tasks and give them a better understanding of their role in the overall organizational mission. To the degree that annual objectives are challenging and provide a sense of purpose, they are also motivational.

Because different units interact with one another, coordination of the annual objectives is an important responsibility of functional area managers. If the annual objective for the sales department is "increase product sales by 12 percent," the production department needs to plan on making 12 percent more product. Backorders, overtime, and lost sales can result from poor coordination between sales and production departments.

BUDGETS

Once well-coordinated annual objectives have been established for the different functional areas, resources need to be allocated to their achievement. Budgets are numerical plans. Within an organization, they represent the projected allocation of resources. Although budgets can be established for the use of labor hours, machine hours, floor space, or other numerically based resources, most budgets are dollar-based.

Budgets are widely applicable to a variety of organizations. Almost everything can be expressed in the single common denominator of dollars. As a result, they are useful for planning activities in such diverse departments as production and marketing research, or at various levels in an organization. Budgets become effective control tools as well as planning tools. They first provide direction and then become the standards against which actual performance can be compared. In fact, the budget is the most widely used planning and controlling tool at every level of an organization.

Types of Budgets

Budgets can be used in many different situations. However some types are more widely used than others. Budgets can be divided into two broad categories. *Financial budgets* spell out in detail the money the organization expects to spend in a particular period and where that money will come from. They include Pro-forma (or estimated) Income Statements, Cash Flow Statements, and Balance Sheets.

Operating budgets indicate, in dollar amounts, the goods and services the organization expects to consume in a budget period. Operating budgets can be developed for a variety of different purposes. The budget types discussed below are examples of operating budgets developed for different purposes.

REVENUE BUDGETS

Revenue budgets are meant to measure marketing and sales effectiveness. They consist of expected quantity of sales multiplied by expected unit selling price. Since quantity, product mix, and in some cases, price are estimates, revenue budgets tend to be the least accurate of the budget types.

When a company has a large number of back orders, such as Volvo, or when its sales are limited by productive capacity rather than ability to sell the product, the revenue budget will be more accurate. Companies operating in a market where supply/demand factors serve to change selling price and units sold frequently will have less reliable revenue budgets. Examples of industries in this situation include most commodities—from oil to peanuts. In these industries, advertising, service, training, and other factors may be used to influence sales in the desired direction.

EXPENSE BUDGETS

While revenue budgets are essentially limited to sales and marketing activities, expense budgets are found in all units within a firm and in both public and private enterprises. They list the primary activities undertaken by a unit and allocate a dollar amount to each. Expense budgets may be used as a measure of efficiency. Exceeding the budget means operating costs were higher than they should have been. When an organization is seeking greater efficiency, it will look at the expense budget to see where less can be spent.

Both fixed and variable costs appear on an expense budget. Fixed costs remain relatively unchanged regardless of the volume of production and might include such factors as interest on capital equipment loans or property taxes. Variable costs tend to rise and fall with volume and include such expenses as shipping and packaging costs, labor costs, and raw materials costs.

PROFIT BUDGETS

A profit budget combines expense and revenue budgets in one statement, sometimes called a master budget. Units in an organization that have clearly delineated revenues are often designated as profit centers and use profit budgets for planning and control. (When a unit does not generate its own revenue, but rather supports a revenue-producing department, a profit budget would not be used. Examples of such departments would include personnel or payroll. Support departments are often referred to as cost centers.)

CASH BUDGETS

Cash budgets bring together the organization's budgeted estimates for revenues, expenses, and new capital expenditures. The budget forecasts how much cash an organization will have on hand and how much it will need to meet expenses. A cash budget deals with the level of funds flowing through the organization, and identifies the pattern of cash disbursements and receipts. This budget can reveal potential shortages or the availability of surplus cash.

Too little cash on hand results in expensive short-term borrowing or loss of discounts for prompt payment of bills. Too much cash on hand results in lost revenues from interest, or may indicate the need for greater capital investment. New businesses just starting out often find themselves in a cash flow bind, whereas IBM must devote significant attention to keeping its substantial cash-on-hand working to earn interest.

CAPITAL EXPENDITURE BUDGETS

Investments in property, buildings, and major equipment are called capital expenditures. A budget that forecasts how much money an organization will invest in these types of items is a capital expenditure budget. Typically, capital expenditures are substantial in both magnitude and duration. Because of the long useful life of buildings and equipment and their relative inflexibility, the choices made on new capital expenditures are not easily altered. As a result, the decisions in the capital expenditure budget are frequently among the more important for an organization. The decision by General Motors to build the new Saturn plant in Tennessee represented a commitment of over $100 million.

VARIABLE AND FIXED BUDGETS

One difficulty with budgets is that they are fixed. As a result, they may be inappropriate, especially in their role as control tools, if situations change in ways beyond the control of those responsible for achieving the budgeted objectives. For example, an expense budget based on annual sales of five million dollars may be completely off track if sales of seven million dollars are achieved. The expenses of manufacturing will increase if more items must be produced to meet the larger demand.

To deal with this difficulty, a variable, or flexible, budget can be developed. Fixed budgets assume a fixed level of sales or production. Variable budgets take into account those costs that vary with volume. In order to develop a variable budget, three types of costs must be taken into account: fixed costs, variable costs, and semivariable costs.

Fixed Costs. Fixed costs are those that are unaffected by the amount of work being done. For example, the insurance premiums on the building are the same whether many units are being produced or very few. As mentioned earlier, property taxes and interest payments are additional examples of fixed costs.

Variable Costs. Variable costs are expenses that vary directly with the amount of work being done. Some examples of variable expenses are supplies, raw materials, inventory taxes, and shipping costs.

Semivariable Costs. Semivariable costs vary with the amount of work performed, but not in a directly proportional way. For example, labor must be hired in blocks, perhaps by the hour or part time. Labor is rarely adjusted on the basis of daily production. A sales staff will not sell the same number of units each day, even though their salaries and benefits will be the same. Such semivariable costs often represent a major portion of an organization's expenses.

In developing variable budgets, fixed costs are separated from variable costs. Variable costs are adjusted for the current level of performance.

Developing Budgets

In the normal budgeting process, the previous year's level of expenditure is assumed to have been appropriate. The task of building the new year's budget is to decide which activities should be dropped and which should be added. Such an incremental process builds in a bias toward continuing the same activities year after year. It makes discovering inefficiencies difficult. It may also encourage inflationary pressures. The incremental process is, however, fast, requiring little managerial time.

PLANNING PROGRAMMING BUDGETING SYSTEM

Originally developed by the Rand Corporation for use by the Air Force, Planning Programming Budgeting System (PPBS) allocates funds to groups of activities or programs that are needed to achieve a specific objective. It was developed to deal with one of the major problems of incremental budgets. Funds are allocated to activities rather than to functional departments. The result is that if a program takes a number of years to complete, PPBS can provide the continuity that is often missing in incremental budgets. The PPBS planning process involves four steps.

1. Set objectives.
2. Establish costs of various programs that could achieve the objectives.
3. Select the most cost-effective programs and allocate program budgets.
4. Evaluate actual program results.

ZERO BASE BUDGETING

Texas Instruments originally developed Zero Base Budgeting (ZBB) in order to circumvent the drawback of incremental budgeting that activities become entrenched. ZBB forces each manager and the organization as a whole to look at its activities and priorities anew. Each manager must justify his or her entire budget request, starting with a base of zero. ZBB has its own set of problems which limit its effectiveness to small public agencies, supporting staffs in business firms, or declining organizations—situations where the benefits far outweigh the costs. The costs of ZBB are a much larger time commitment, greater analysis of data, more paperwork, and artificial inflation of a project's importance,

SCHEDULING

Supervisors and department managers regularly detail what activities have to be done, the order they are to be done in, when they are to be completed, and who is responsible for completing them. Fortunately, several useful scheduling tools have been developed to help managers, or all managers might sound like Debbi, the manager of a college coffee shop. When Barbara applied to work at the coffee shop, Debbi agreed to hire her. Barbara asked when she'd be working. Debbi said she'd give her a call. Barbara asked if there wasn't a regular work schedule. Debbi said she didn't believe in scheduling because every time she made a schedule, someone would be sick or have an exam, so she just didn't make schedules anymore.

Debbi's approach to managing will not work as the tasks become more complex and numerous. Building hydroelectric power plants, scheduling automobile assembly lines, and preparing monthly American Express billings are all examples of the major scheduling problems which face organizations. As the expected use of equipment, space, or human resources approaches maximum capacity, the need for better scheduling also increases.

Gantt Chart

Henry Gantt developed the chart that bears his name around the turn of the century. Essentially, it is a bar chart with time on the horizontal axis and activities to be scheduled on the vertical axis.

The chart provides a visual picture of when tasks are supposed to be done and the actual progress being made on each. Gantt Charts are used when the number of activities being scheduled is limited and when the tasks are independent of each other. Because Gantt Charts are easy to prepare, they provide managers with an inexpensive tool for determining whether a project is ahead, behind, or on schedule. Most Gantt Charts use movable strips of plastic, with different colors to indicate scheduled and actual progress. Boards with movable pegs or cards are also used. A student with multiple courses might use a Gantt Chart to schedule class assignments throughout a term.

Program Evaluation and Review Technique

The Program Evaluation and Review Technique (PERT) was developed by the Navy in the 1950s. When a project requires hundreds or even thousands of activities, some of which must be done simultaneously and some of which cannot begin until earlier activities have been completed, PERT is a helpful scheduling tool. Using PERT is sometimes referred to as the Critical Path Method (CPM), because it warns managers if a critical event is behind schedule.

Managers of political campaigns use them, as do construction companies and project managers. A PERT network is a flowchart that depicts the sequence of activities needed to complete a project and the time or costs associated with each activity. It aids in scheduling by focusing attention on key project steps and by pointing to potential problem areas.

Timing and sequencing are the primary concerns in a PERT network. The steps in constructing a network include the following:

1. Identifying and defining the component activities that must be performed. In the building of a house, component activities would include such jobs as foundation work, framing, wiring, plumbing, siding, plastering, painting interior, painting exterior, cabinet work, and cleanup.

2. Defining the order in which those activities in the network will be performed. In building the house, the foundation must be completed before the framing. However, the plumbing and wiring can be done at essentially the same time.

3. Determining the estimated time required to complete the individual activities and the entire project. A contractor might plan two weeks for foundation work and only two days for interior sheetrock work.

4. Finding the critical path—the longest path, in terms of time, from the beginning event to the ending event. If a delay occurs in any of the events along the critical path, the entire project will take longer than planned. Managers keep a careful eye on the critical path, so they can take corrective action early if something goes wrong. If the building inspector must approve the foundation work before framing can begin, and the inspector is ill, then perhaps additional framers will need to be hired to keep the job on schedule.

5. Improving on the initial plan through modifications. Perhaps a "make versus buy" decision is called for. Should the cabinet work be done by a cabinet shop or by on-site carpenters? Which would take the least time? Would either

decision affect the critical path? Would either result in a better quality job?

6. Controlling the project. A PERT network is merely a scheduling tool. Writing down activities and probable times for completing them is not the same as seeing that they get done. As a result, the manager must control the project to keep it on track.

Break-Even Analysis

How many units of a product must an organization sell in order to break even, or have neither a profit nor a loss? Break-even analysis is a technique for identifying the point at which total revenue is equal to total costs. In addition to demonstrating the number of units that must be made and sold, break-even analysis can provide information about whether a particular product should continue to be sold or be dropped from the organization's product line. Mathematically, the break-even point in units can be determined by dividing the total fixed costs by sales price per unit minus the variable cost per unit.

$$\text{Break even point} = \frac{\text{fixed costs}}{(\text{unit sales price}) - \text{unit variable costs}}$$

Break-even analysis might also help in setting an appropriate price. In Lee Iacocca's 1984 autobiography, he says that in 1979, Chrysler had to sell 2.3 million vehicles to break even. After three years of stringent cost reduction and reorganization, the break-even point had been reduced to 1.1 million units.

Linear Programming

Linear Programming (LP) is a mathematical technique that solves resource allocation problems. It is especially appropriate in situations where resources are limited and a variety of possible combinations of resources exist. LP will assist the manager in choosing the optimal allocation. For example, a paint company has three paint mixing machines and one shipping department. They make a latex paint that has a profit margin of $4000/batch and an enamel paint which has a profit margin of $5000/batch. The latex paint, including set-up, takes 2 days per batch in mixing and .5 day in shipping, while the enamel paint takes 3 days per batch in mixing and .5 day in shipping. How much of each type of paint would result in the most profitable product mix? Maximum profit, the objective function, can be expressed as $4000L + $5000E, where L is the number of batches of latex and E is the number of batches of enamel.

Linear programming is actually the analysis of constraints. In the paint example, the constraints are the total number of mixing days available and the total number of shipping days available. Assuming the company operates all three machines for a total of 300 days per year, 900 mixing days is capacity. If the shipping department works only four days per week, 208 shipping days is that department's capacity. Therefore, production capacity numbers act as constraints on overall capacity. The constraint equations are as follows:

$$2L + 3E \geq 900$$
$$.5L + .5E \geq 208$$

If only latex is made, maximum profit is $1.664 million. If only enamel in made, maximum profit is $1.5 million. However, if 348 batches of latex and 68 batches of enamel are made, maximum profit is $1.732 million.

Queuing Theory

Queuing theory, frequently called waiting-line theory, is a technique that balances the costs of having a service line open against the costs of having customers waiting. Queuing theory is used by McDonald's to determine how many cash registers are needed, by Bank of America to determine the number of teller windows, and by Delta Airlines to determine the number of airline ticket counters that should be open during a particular period. The mathematics of queuing theory are beyond the scope of this book. However, the logic is that customers will wait patiently only so long. It takes some time to assist each customer. Suppose a person can be expected to wait twelve minutes. If it takes four minutes to help each customer, then no line can get longer than four customers. If the rate of arrival of customers averages two per minute, then there would be a one in sixteen chance of a line becoming longer than three people.

While studying queuing theory and its applications, researchers discovered that as long as customers are "making progress" in a line, they are willing to wait longer. Putting customers in one long line, rather than several short lines, gives customers the sense that they are moving along rapidly. It also reduces the jealousy that results when someone who enters last is served first because his or her line moves faster. Most service-line situations now use the single waiting-line approach.

Sampling Theory

Sampling theory applies statistical probability analysis to situations in order to analyze patterns and reduce the need to test each individual product for quality. In quality control, there is a trade-off between the costs of testing a product and the costs of letting a bad product out of the factory. In some cases, testing the product makes it useless (as in crash-testing automobiles for safety.) In those situations, the cost of testing is very high. In some cases, not testing every product is too expensive, as Cutter Laboratories found out. They released a batch of polio vaccine that was not inactive—many children contracted the disease from the vaccine. Most situations fall in the middle, and the manufacturer must determine how frequently testing needs to be done. Based on past patterns, sampling theory provides the manager with two probabilities: (1) the probability that a bad product will be sold, and (2) the probability that a good product will be held back. Armed with these two figures, the manager can make quality testing schedules.

Simulation

A simulation is a model of a real situation. Variables in the model can be manipulated and the result observed. As a simple example, managers may move paper cutouts of equipment around on a scale drawing of a room to determine the best arrangement. Computer simulation has allowed the models and the number of changeable variables to become very complex. Flight simulators are examples of extremely complex models. While flight simulators might cost millions of dollars, they are still a less expensive way of training pilots than putting them in the air. Several simulation languages have been developed to assist computer programmers in simulation modeling. As a result, simulation is becoming more widely used every day. Like linear programming, simulation can help managers decide the most profitable or productive use of a variety of resources.

TIME MANAGEMENT

Time management is personal scheduling—operational planning on the individual level. Since time, once gone, cannot be recovered, and since time is a resource equally distributed to everyone, its thoughtful use can become a differential advantage for a manager.

According to Stephen Covey in *The Seven Habits of Highly Effective People*, activities may be thought of as falling into one of four quadrants: (1) those activities that are important and urgent, such as deadline driven projects and crises; (2) those activities which are important and not urgent, such as planning and building relationships; (3) those activities that are urgent but not important, such as interruptions, some phone calls, and some meetings; and (4) those activities that are neither important nor urgent, such as watching television and wasting time.

Unless they give thought to how they use their time, managers will find they spend all their time reacting to urgent situations, many of which are not really important. The goal is to reduce time spent on urgent, crisis situations because they result in stress, burnout, a short-term focus, and crisis management. The following steps assist in moving activities from urgent, stress-generating times to important, but not urgent times. The result should be vision, perspective, balance, discipline, and control. As a consequence, the number of crises will be significantly reduced.

Steps to Effective Time Management

In order to take control of time, a manager needs know what he or she wants to accomplish and how important each activity is. Personal time management is much like organizational planning. As Covey says, "start with the end in mind."

1. Write a personal mission statement. A mission statement provides a solid foundation or grounding to an individual as well as to an organization.

2. Make a list of objectives. Each individual plays several roles, within the family, the organization, and the community. Each role requires clear, time-specific objectives. In the managerial role, the objectives might include unit or team objectives as well as individual objectives.

3. Rank the list of objectives. Not everything is of equal importance. Assigning priorities is an important time-management step.

4. List the activities necessary to reach the objectives. Small activities are easier to accomplish than large objectives.

5. For each objective, assign priorities, paying special attention to activities that are important but not urgent. Goethe said, "Things which matter most must never be at the mercy of things which matter least." Giving those activities which are important, but not urgent, highest priority will make the greatest difference in effective time management.

6. Schedule weekly activities to reflect activity priorities. Scheduling by the week rather than by the day, and scheduling in activities that reflect objectives in each role will assure movement away from crisis management. Most people have productivity cycles—times during the day when they are most productive and times when their energy is low. Scheduling both manager and subordinate time to take daily energy cycles into consideration is a good idea.

Reaching organizational objectives requires two kinds of planning— strategic planning to identify organizational strengths and mission, and operational planning to implement the strategy. Budgeting and scheduling tools are available to make operational planning both more effective and more efficient.

In addition to serving as planning tools, budgets and schedules serve as control tools. They set the goals to which actual performance can be compared.

Although computers are typically used to handle the actual mathematical calculations required by budgeting and scheduling tools, understanding the uses and weaknesses of the various techniques will assist managers in applying them correctly. A tool is only as good as the application to which it is put.

Time management is operational planning on an individual level. As a result, effective time management begins with establishing a personal mission and relevant objectives. The manager who makes effective use of time will reduce both personal and organizational stress.

Selected Readings

Camp, Roger. 1987. "Multidimensional Break–even Analysis." *Journal of Accountancy* 154: 132–133.

Churchill, Neil. 1984. "Budget Choice: Planning vs. Control." *Harvard Business Review* 62: 150–166.

Covey, Stephen. 1989. *The Seven Habits of Highly Effective People*. New York: Simon and Shuster.

Fearon, Harold, William Ruch, Vincent Reuter, David Wieters, and Ross Reck. 1986. *Foundations of Production/Operations Management*, 3rd ed. St. Paul, MN: West Publishing.

Klammer, Thomas, and Michael Walker. 1984. "The Continuing Increase in the Use of Sophisticated Capital Budgeting Techniques." *California Management Review* 27: 137–148.

Lindquist, Stanton, and Bryant Mills. 1981. "Whatever Happened to Zero Based Budgeting?" *Managerial Planning* 29: 31–35.

Mackenzie, R. A. 1975. *The Time Trap*. New York: McGraw-Hill.

Stiansen, Sarah. 1988. "Breaking Even." *Success* Nov: 17–19.

Umpathy, Srinivasan. 1987. "How Successful Firms Budget." *Management Accounting* 69: 25–27.

Weatherbee, James and John Montanari. 1981. "Zero-Base Budgeting in the Planning Process." *Strategic Management Journal* Mar: 1–14.

10

Organizing Organizations: Concepts and Designs

B*uckminster Fuller said that in good architectural design, form follows function. One first decides what the function or purpose of a building or a room is, and then lets the function dictate the shape of the building or room. In good organizational design, structure follows strategy. After the strategy is determined, then an appropriate structure is developed.*

Organizations are a collection of human and capital resources. In order for the resources to function as an efficient whole, they need to be structured or organized—work needs to be arranged and allocated among members of the organization. Methods for coordinating the various members need to be developed.

The organizing process involves balancing the need for stability with the need for change and the need for division with the need for coordination. This chapter discusses several aspects of organizational structure: division of work, departmentalization, coordination, and organizational design.

ORGANIZING

Certain questions of design must be addressed by all organizations. Each organization needs to consider (1) how work tasks will be grouped into jobs, (2) how jobs will be combined into departments, (3) how decision-making authority will be dispersed, (4) how many subordinates each manager will supervise, and (5) how different activities will be coordinated. An organization's strategy, objectives, technology, size, and environment will all influence what constitutes the most effective answer to these questions of design.

First, each of the general topics of design will be discussed. Once the foundation is set, consideration will be given to how internal and external environmental factors influence choices within the design elements.

JOB DESIGN

A job can be defined as the group of tasks one person has responsibility for accomplishing. In the typical organization, there may be millions of individual tasks which need to be completed. There are an infinite number of ways of combining all those tasks into jobs. Not surprisingly, some of the ways are better than others.

The Job Characteristics Model

The job characteristics model, originally developed by Richard Hackman and Greg Oldham, offers a conceptual framework for designing jobs. According to this model, any job can be described in terms of five core dimensions.

> *Skill variety* is the degree to which a job requires a variety of activities and a number of different skills and talents.

> *Task identity* is the degree to which a job requires completion on a whole and identifiable piece of work.

> *Task significance* is the degree to which a job has a substantial impact on the lives or work of other people.

> *Autonomy* is the degree to which a job provides substantial freedom, independence, and discretion to the job holder in scheduling the work and determining the procedures to be used in carrying it out.

> *Feedback* is the degree to which carrying out the work activities required by a job results in the job holder's obtaining clear and direct information about the effectiveness of his or her performance.

Assembly-line work tends to be low on all the core dimensions except feedback. Frequently, the next step in the assembly cannot be undertaken if the previous step was not completed perfectly. Teaching, on the other hand, is high on all the other dimensions but low on feedback. Teachers rarely know how much they have actually taught someone.

The job characteristics model predicts that certain job designs are more motivating than others. The following suggestions would be most likely to lead to improvements in each of the five core dimensions.

1. Combine tasks. Jobs made up of highly specialized tasks should be combined. This increases skill variety and task identity.

2. Create natural work units. When tasks are combined such that an identifiable whole exists, workers are encouraged to view their work as meaningful and important.

3. Establish client relationships. A direct relationship between the user of the product or service and the employee who creates it increases skill variety, autonomy, task identity, and feedback.

4. Expand jobs vertically. Essentially, vertical expansion means giving the employee the job of managing his or her own task. It closes the gap between doing a job and controlling or supervising the job. As a result, it increases worker autonomy.

5. Open feedback channels. The more feedback a worker receives and the faster it is received, the more able a worker is to learn how well he or she is doing and take corrective action when necessary.

Job Specialization

Specialization of labor is the division of a complex activity into jobs that contain only a few tasks so that one person carries out only identical or related activities. Specialization of labor allows workers to become experts, or specialists, in a particular area. The skill and knowledge level of the worker tends to be much higher. On an automobile assembly line, for example, a worker with a highly specialized job may only mount the front and rear left wheels.

Adam Smith originally described the power of specialization of labor in *The Wealth of Nations*. Smith had been to watch sewing pin makers. Wire was heated, drawn to a sharp point and cut, a glass or metal head was manufactured and then attached, the pins were counted and placed on cards or in boxes. A pin maker performed all the steps or tasks in the pin-making process. Smith was able to increase the productivity of the group of pin makers a thousand times through specialization. He reorganized the tasks, and one person tended the fires, another heated and pulled the wire, another cut it, another made pin heads, another attached them, and yet another boxed them.

ADVANTAGES OF SPECIALIZATION

In general, specialization has several advantages. It increases productivity, as Adam Smith discovered. It allows one supervisor to supervise more subordinates because they are all doing the same job and so the complexity of the supervising job is lower (the managerial job becomes more specialized as well). Training time is reduced. Typically, specialization results in higher product quality.

DISADVANTAGES OF SPECIALIZATION

Even though the advantages of specialization can be impressive, jobs that have low task variety are boring and can lead to fatigue. Carpal tunnel syndrome, a pain or numbing of the hands, is caused by the repetitive motions of keyboarding or scanning. Carpal tunnel syndrome is the fastest-growing work-related injury. Too much specialization leads to a high level of employee turnover and absenteeism. Quality may decline.

Job Rotation

One of the simplest ways to combat the disadvantages of specialization is job rotation. The jobs remain highly specialized. However, workers move from job to job to diversify their activities and avoid boredom. Many organizations formalize job rotation, regularly moving employees from one job to the next.

The advantages of job rotation are many. Job rotation broadens employees and gives them a range of skills, reducing boredom and monotony. It also allows them to see the interrelationships of activities and how one job effects another. The organization has greater flexibility when an employee is sick or leaves the company. Of course, training costs are higher and accidents may increase.

Job Enlargement

Job enlargement is a simple approach to changing job design. Several very specialized jobs are combined into one. The resultant job contains a greater number of different operations. The automobile assembly-line worker may be responsible for spin balancing the tire/wheel assemblies before bolting them to the car.

Job enlargement is not particularly successful, because the only core job dimension affected by it is task variety. If the tasks are relatively specialized and uninteresting, more of them will not be seen as an advantage.

Job Enrichment

Job enrichment is the vertical expansion of a job by adding planning or controlling tasks. Essentially, job enrichment allows employees greater control over their work. Each job includes some degree of managing responsibility. The tasks in an enriched job allow workers to do a complete activity with increased freedom, independence, and responsibility. More of the core job dimensions are increased.

Pacific Bell, the California telephone company, applied job enrichment to the tasks of preparing the Yellow Pages Directory. Originally, the process was very specialized. A salesperson made the contact with potential advertisers. A design consultant met with customers. The typesetting department set the copy. Copyeditors checked for accuracy. Under the enriched system, one directory representative is given full responsibility for a section of the Yellow Pages. That representative contacts potential clients, helps them prepare their ads, checks the ads for accuracy, and works with the same clients the next year. As a result of having full responsibility for one section, the representative has a better sense of what the section will look like, what kinds of ads will fit in, and what the customers need to say about themselves. The representatives like their work more because they can see the finished product, and the customers believe they are getting a better product. Copy errors are way down and advertising sales are way up since the job redesign took effect.

Work Teams

Tasks can be grouped into an individual job or into a team job. Work teams are groups of individuals who cooperate to complete a set of tasks. Fully autonomous work teams even select their own members and have the members evaluate one another's performance. The General Motors Saturn factory uses a team concept, somewhat unusual in mass-produced automobiles. In some industries, team work is the usual. For example, Apple Computers uses teams for all its design, programming, and marketing functions.

Job Scheduling

When workers work is an additional element of job design. More and more organizations are incorporating alternatives to the standard eight-hour work shift. One such alternative is the compressed work week.

COMPRESSED WORK WEEK

The compressed work week is typically composed of four ten-hour workdays. At least in the short run, compressed workweeks have several advantages. They provide employees with more leisure time, decrease commuting time, decrease requests for personal time off, and have a favorable effect on employee satisfaction and productivity. In the long run, the compressed workweek may result in increased fatigue, greater scheduling problems, reduced customer service, and underutilized equipment.

FLEXTIME

Flexible work hours, sometimes called flextime, is a scheduling system in which employees are required to work a certain number of hours per week, but are free within limits to vary the actual hours of work. Most flextime programs require all employees to be at work for certain core periods, perhaps from 10:00 a.m. to 2:00 p.m. The office can be open from 6:00 a.m. to 6:00 p.m., allowing some workers to arrive early while others will choose to remain late. Not all jobs can be adapted to flextime scheduling. However, the response to flextime is very positive, with improved moral and improved worker productivity. In geographical areas where the commuting problem is significant, flextime is especially helpful.

JOB SHARING

Job sharing allows two or more people to split a traditional full-time job. Such a program allows organizations to get the knowledge and talents of two people rather than one. A certain number of highly skilled potential employees are unwilling to work full time. Job sharing is a boon for them and the companies who hire them. Typically, benefits are more expensive for companies who offer job sharing programs.

CONTINGENT WORKERS

According to the *Wall Street Journal*, temporary and part-time workers now represent 30 percent of the workforce, and their number is growing at the rate of 20 percent annually. Temporaries provide flexibility to organizations. They allow organizations to boost productivity in boom times and avoid the bad publicity of layoffs during slow times. For some workers, temporary and part-time work suits them perfectly—allowing them greater autonomy and diversity. For many, however, contingent-worker status is demoralizing.

TELECOMMUTING

Personal computers connected by phone lines allow many workers to work from home. The latest figures indicate that 30 million workers work at least some time from home. The number of full-time telecommuters is probably closer to 12 million and includes programmers, researchers, writers, purchasers, designers, and many other white-collar occupations.

The advantages of working at home, in terms of reduced environmental impact, are significant. Telecommuters do not drive to work, nor do they need parking spaces. They do not require special business clothes. Major office buildings do not need to be constructed to "house" them. In fact, the energy required to power one telephone line for data transmission is so low it is almost not measurable. Telecommuting is a special boon to handicapped workers and to workers with small children or elderly parents who need occasional assistance.

Telecommuting does not, however, fit the traditional description of being part of an organization. Supervising the telecommuter is different from supervising a subordinate who is on-site. Social contacts are reduced. Political relationships are less likely to develop. In order to reap the benefits to worker and organization which telecommuting offers, changes in organizational structure will need to occur.

DEPARTMENTATION

Once tasks are combined into jobs, the jobs need to be combined into units or departments. This step in the organizational design process is called departmentation. Departmentation is an important element in coordinating activities. Several standard approaches to departmentation have arisen over the years. An organization chooses among them by considering which approach would contribute the most to efficiently coordinating activities. The answers to the following questions will assist the organization in making the choice.

1. Is the volume of a certain type of work large enough to justify having it in its own department?

2. Do tradition, preferences, or work rules support a particular department type?

3. Do conflicts of interest exist that departmentation could reduce?

4. Do similar functions need to be completed in a variety of different systems in the organization?

5. Would combining dissimilar functions improve coordination?

Departmentation by Function

The most common way to combine jobs is by function. Under this approach, departments are formed by grouping together jobs on the basis of specialized activities or functions. A manufacturing plant might have departments of purchasing, product design, lathe work, milling work, finishing, shipping, finance, personnel, and marketing. A hospital might have departments of admitting, records, payroll, nursing, housekeeping, and staff physicians. When people with similar training and similar work problems work together, they can assist each other easily. The benefits of specialization are realized.

Departmentation by Product

Especially when a company is quite large and its product line is quite disparate, grouping jobs according to product may offer certain advantages. For example, a company which produces a full range of computers might choose to have a division responsible for personal computers, and another in charge of the mainframe operations. Each division would resemble a separate business with its own departments of finance, marketing, etc. This type of departmentation allows the division to specialize according to product, customer, or market, rather than by functional area.

Departmentation by Customer

Similar to a product division organization is a customer or market departmentation approach. Aircraft manufacturers may have a division for commercial customers and another for military contracts. Although the products are similar, the needs of the these two customers are very different, for example, in terms of proposals, bids, cost justifications, and security. Organizing by customer or market allows the company to provide service tailormade to customer needs.

Departmentation by Territory

When an organization operates over a large geographic territory, grouping activities by region may provide special advantages. Especially when values and needs are quite different among the territories, regional departments encourage an organization to focus on the differences, thus providing more appropriate products and services. The Broadway is a department store that operates in the West. The Southwest region is a different division, complete with a different name—Broadway Southwest. The chain decided on this division when sales proved to be much lower than expected in the Southwest. Customers in Arizona and New Mexico prefer to buy home furnishings such as towels, sheets, and pillows in desert colors—pinks, browns, and golds. The Broadway's customers in California and Washington prefer their home furnishings in blues, greens, and whites. Centralized buying and merchandising had not worked. Once The Broadway departmentalized by territory, sales grew.

ORGANIZATIONAL STRUCTURE

Span of Control

An important variable in organizational design is how many subordinates one supervisor manages. This element is called span of control or span of management. The most effective span depends on the kind of jobs being supervised, how critical quality control is, how skilled the workers are, how autonomous the jobs are, how skilled the manager is, and how centralized decision making is in the organization. A department manager in a university may easily supervise sixty faculty members, because the faculty are largely independent contractors. Alternatively, many of the jobs at NASA have a span of control of one! A supervisor supervises the work of only one person, because quality control is absolutely critical.

Although the span of control will not be consistent throughout an organization, some organizations will tend toward narrow spans of control; others will tend toward wide spans. Over an entire organization, the span of control determines the number of levels of management. When each supervisor supervises ten workers, an organization of one hundred and one people requires only two managerial levels. However if no manager supervises over three people, four levels of management would be required, making the organization appear "taller" on an organization chart.

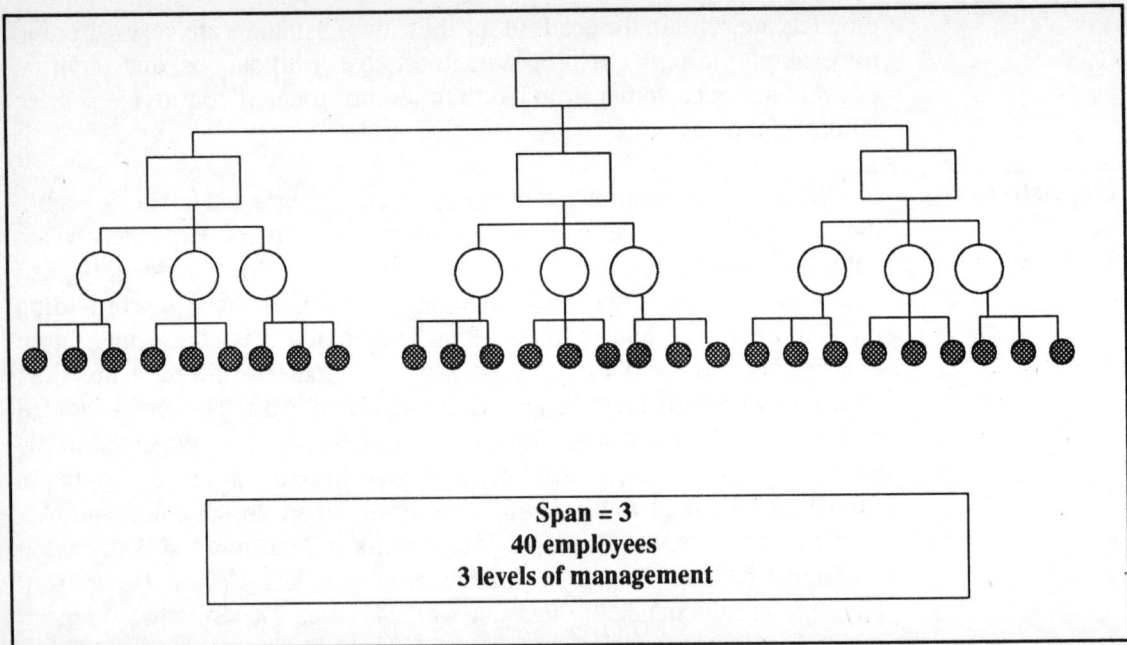

Span = 3
40 employees
3 levels of management

Fig. 10.1 Span of Control: Span = 3

A major direction in organization structuring is movement toward wider spans of control and fewer levels of management. Workers tend to prefer the degree of self-management a wider span requires of them, and organizations gain the efficiency of having less overhead.

Unity of Command

In addition to considering the number of subordinates each manager supervises, organization design considers the number of managers each employee reports to. Fayol's Classical Management Theory argued that unity of command was critical to good organization. Unity of command means that each worker has one and only one supervisor. The modern matrix and network organizations, which will be discussed in detail later in this chapter, consistently break the unity of command principle. Workers are likely to report to two or three different managers as a regular part of their jobs.

Strategy and Structure

In 1962, Alfred Chandler published a landmark study of the relationship between structure and strategy in 100 large U. S. companies. Based on their histories, Chandler concluded that changes in corporate strategy precede, and lead to, changes in organizational structure. He proposed that as companies move from single product to vertical integration to product diversification, structure will move from a more open, flexible one to a more mechanical, centralized one. Recent research has supported the finding that certain strategies are better supported by certain structures.

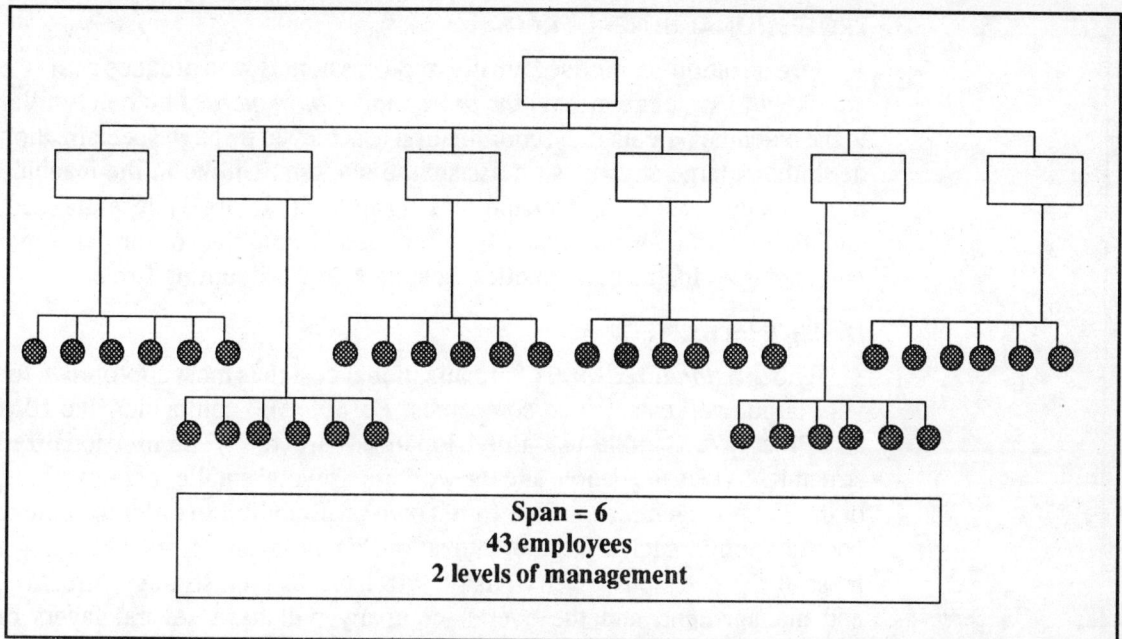

Span = 6
43 employees
2 levels of management

Fig. 10.2 Span of Control: Span = 6

SIMPLE STRUCTURE

Most small and young organizations are pursuing a survival and growth strategy. According to research by Henry Mintzberg, organizations pursuing this strategy should use a simple structure wherein coordination of activities is maintained by a manager who directly supervises the production employees. Tasks tend not to be specialized, and the owner retains the decision-making authority. Because of its small size and simple structure, the organization can change quickly with the environment. Start-up companies and small to medium size retail stores tend to follow this strategy and structure.

MACHINE BUREAUCRACY

When an organization is large, its product line is well established, and it is taking a slow-growth strategy, the *machine bureaucracy* structure is probably most appropriate. The machine bureaucracy structure is likely to have highly specialized jobs using an assembly-line technology. Spans of control are narrow. Authority and decision making follow a rigid unity of command. Policies and procedures are usually very detailed, with few exceptions allowed. The structure allows the organization to focus on increasing efficiency and quality. Companies most likely to follow this strategy and structure would include container manufacturers, the U. S. Postal Service, and steel companies.

PROFESSIONAL BUREAUCRACY

Organizations comprised mostly of professionals who produce a service are likely to structure around the *professional bureaucracy* model. Similar to the machine bureaucracy, coordination is achieved through specialization of skills. A large support staff assists the workers. Unlike in the machine bureaucracy, though, the decision-making authority is largely decentralized, and middle management is often reduced. Examples of professional bureaucracies include universities, hospitals, and accounting firms.

DIVISIONALIZED FORM

The *divisionalized form* of organizational design is most appropriate for very large, well established companies. *Fortune* 500 companies like IBM and Procter & Gamble use a divisionalized structure. The divisionalized structure divides the people and the work into several smaller organizations, or divisions—each responsible for its own profitability. In order to achieve coordination in such a large organization, many layers of managers make most of the decisions. Each division will have its own strategy, structure, and management, and the overall company will have several layers of management in addition.

ADHOCRACY

When an organization wishes to emphasize innovation and adaptation, the *adhocracy* model of organization will provide the best results.This structure emphasizes coordination through mutual agreement, and avoids formality, specialization, and centralized authority. Typically, such organizations operate in environments that are dynamic and complex. Apple Computer, Cellular One, and Merck are examples of companies whose strategy suggests the adhocracy model of organizing.

Size and Structure

The size of an organization, especially when measured by number of employees, influences its structure. As the number of employees increases, the organization becomes less flexible, the jobs become more specialized, more departments are created, and more decisions are made at lower managerial levels. According to research, this influence of size on structure holds true until an organization has about 2000 employees. After that point, size does not appear to make much difference.

Environment and Structure

In 1961, Tom Burns and G. M. Stalker provided the first research to demonstrate a relationship between an organization's external environment and its structure. Since their work, others have added to the data, which suggests that complex and rapidly changing environments call for a different structure from more stable environments.

STABLE ENVIRONMENTS

When a company produces a very similar product year after year, using very similar technology, and the customer is pleased with that, a stable environment exists. Manufacturers of paper products or fertilizers operate within a fairly unchanging environment. In such a situation, organizations can be structured in a *mechanistic* way. The mechanistic organizational form includes the following structural elements.

1. Tasks are specialized.

2. Tasks are rigidly defined.

3. Strict unity of command is followed.

4. Rules are numerous.

5. Control of tasks is centralized at top of organization.

6. Communication is vertical.

RAPIDLY CHANGING ENVIRONMENTS

When technology, products, customers, or resources change frequently, an organization is operating in a complex, rapidly changing environment. Medical care, for example, is provided in a rapidly changing environment. Computers and communication technologies are making the economic environment in general more complex. In such environments, an *organic* organizational form will be more appropriate. An organic organization has the following characteristics.

1. Teamwork is common.

2. Tasks are adjusted through employee interaction.

3. Rules are few.

4. Hierarchy is flexible.

5. Control of tasks is located throughout organization.

6. Communication is horizontal.

Paul Lawrence and Jay Lorsch identified two additional structural dimensions necessary to organizations that function in rapidly changing environments. In order to develop expertise and handle environmental uncertainty, organizations need to increase their differentiation. Differentiation is the extent to which the organization is broken down into departments that differ by managers' orientations.

Because frequent change requires more information processing and adjustments within and across departments, organizations in rapidly changing environments also need increased integration. Integration is the degree of collaboration that exists among departments.

Technology and Structure

Technology—the ideas, machinery, techniques, and actions an organization uses to create its product or service—has a significant influence on organizational strategy. In 1965, Joan Woodward observed that the technology in manufacturing firms influenced their structure. She identified three classes of technology and the resultant structures.

UNIT, OR SMALL-BATCH TECHNOLOGY

Firms that use this technology might also be called job shops. They set up their equipment or human resources differently for each job or client. Automobile repair facilities, hospitals, and hair salons use unit or small batch technology. The structure that results from this technology is more open and flexible. Teamwork will be common and the number of managerial levels will be low. The amount of verbal communication is typically high, while the amount of written communication is low.

MASS-PRODUCTION , OR LARGE-BATCH TECHNOLOGY

With large-batch technology, the transformation process is performed typically in assembly-line fashion. Long production runs using standardized parts are usual, and the product is standardized as well. Some typical examples of this production technology include automobile assembly, canned food processing, and textile manufacture. Large-batch technology is best suited to a high degree of specialization, quite centralized decision making, a great deal of formal written communication, and little verbal communication. The mechanistic bureaucracy is typical.

CONTINUOUS-PROCESS TECHNOLOGY

Continuous-process technology is almost fully automated. Machines handle the production process almost entirely and turn out a uniform product. Stopping and starting the process are very difficult and expensive. Chemical refineries, hydroelectric power plants, and flour mills are examples of organizations that use this technology. The structure most typical of continuous-process includes many managerial levels, highly skilled workers who make decisions, a high degree of verbal communication, and little written communication.

Woodward's study focused on manufacturing firms. Management scholar Charles Perrow identified a broader framework, which he believed would apply to all organizations. He proposed that technology be viewed in terms of two dimensions.

1. Task variability—the number of exceptions individuals encounter in their work. For example, a store may have a "satisfaction guaranteed" policy, which store clerks interpret to mean "give customers a refund if they request it." However, when a customer brings back an obviously worn-

out item and requests a refund, the clerk has to make a decision about how to interpret the policy. The more exceptions a worker experiences, the greater the task variability.

2. Problem analyzability—the type of problem-solving procedures available to individuals in responding to these exceptions. As an example, automobile mechanics have a greater number of problem-solving options than assemblers of stereo components.

Using these two dimensions, Perrow constructed a matrix identifying four types of technology.

ROUTINE TECHNOLOGIES

Routine technologies have few exceptions and easy-to-analyze problems. Mass-production processes belong in this category. Because the technology is routine, the structure can be standardized. Organizations can rely on procedures and rules to limit the decision-making latitude in a highly mechanistic organization.

ENGINEERING TECHNOLOGIES

Engineering technologies have a large number of exceptions, but they can be handled in a rational and systemized manner. Highway construction or drug research fall in this category. Policies will help low-level decision makers in a more decentralized structure.

CRAFT TECHNOLOGIES

Craft technologies deal with relatively difficult problems but with a limited set of exceptions. Cabinet makers and dentists are examples of people who use craft technologies.

NONROUTINE TECHNOLOGIES

The technologies which fall in the nonroutine category are characterized by many exceptions and by difficult-to-analyze problems. This technology requires the least standardized structure, with much more verbal communication than written communication. Teamwork and an organic structure would be the norm with this category of technologies. Building a space telescope or working on superconductivity would require nonroutine technology.

CURRENT TOPICS IN ORGANIZATIONAL DESIGN

Rapidly changing technologies and an increasingly complex environment are leading organizations to try new structures. Two structures are being applied more and more—matrix and network.

Matrix Organization

In the late 1960s, the aerospace industry was under pressure by the government which demanded that military contractors appoint a single contract manager for each project. The project manager would be responsible to the government for the project's progress. To meet the government requirement, a project leader was established who shared authority with the managers of the pre-existing functional departments. This temporary arrangement has evolved into a widely used "matrix" organization. In a matrix organization, each employee reports to both a functional or division manager and to a project manager.

If an employee's functional area is accounting, he will have an accounting supervisor. At different times in his work career, he will be a member of different project teams. During this year, he may serve as the accountant for a team that is designing a computerized information system for a client. Next year, he may be the accountant for a team that solves an internal work scheduling problem.

As a market researcher, an employee will have a supervisor from the marketing functional area. She will also be supervised by the project leader of a new product development group.

The matrix design is an efficient way to bring together the many specialized skills necessary to solve complex problems. It increases coordination and flexibility. Because an effective matrix structure requires personal flexibility and cooperation from organizational members, not everyone likes working in one. Good interpersonal relationship skills are also required in a matrix structure.

The Network Structure

A new form of organizational design is currently gaining popularity. The network structure is a small centralized organization that relies on other organizations to perform its basic business functions on a contract basis. Pacific Gas and Electric, a major power supply company on the West Coast, is moving toward a network structure. The company has released its entire construction division. When a new power plant needs to be constructed, the company will put the job out for bid. They have released many of the training and development staff, preferring to contract for training services. Electronic Data Services (EDS) is a company that has grown rapidly by providing payroll and tax preparation services for network-designed companies.

Some researchers have referred to the network structure as "the hollow corporation." In essence, managers in network structures spend most of their time coordinating and controlling *external* relations.

The network structure is ideal for strategies that require very high flexibility in order to respond quickly to fads, for example, in toy companies, or to fashion, for example in women's clothing. When a product is no longer selling well, the network company simply drops its contract with the supplier. Since the company owns no manufacturing facilities and employs no production workers, dropping a product line has almost no associated costs. The network structure is also specially suited to firms that contract with low-wage foreign suppliers. When changes in the value of the dollar or shipping costs make one foreign supplier better than another, the company can simply change its contracts.

Disadvantages might include loss of control over manufacturing operations, low supplies reliability, and low security of company innovations.

Amoeba Structure

Many organizations are using a structure called *organic appendages*, which combines a rather traditional, functionally-organized core with amoeba-like appendages that form and reform as needed. These organizations incorporate into their structures hybrid project teams—organizational members join with members of other organizations. For example, MicroSoft and IBM developed the "Windows" software as a joint project. Employees from both companies joined a temporary minicompany.

At any one time, Applied Materials, a manufacturer of silicon chip-making machines, has 300 employees working on-site at customers' or suppliers' factories. The employees are paid by Applied Materials, but they are supervised by managers at the factories where they work. According to Rosabeth Moss Kanter, editor of *Harvard Business Review*, this flowing organizational design will become typical of future organizations. The increasingly complex business environment will demand organizational flexibility beyond what traditional structures can produce.

Once an organization has set its strategy, it must design a structure that will help it reach its strategic objectives. Strategy, technology, size, and environment all influence the appropriate organizational design. When an organization's strategy changes, the structural elements of the organization must change as well.

The structural elements over which the organization has control include job design, departmentation, span of control, unity of command, coordination, and authority relationships. Coordination will be discussed further in chapter 18—Communicating. The next chapter looks in greater depth at the subject of authority relationships.

Selected Readings

Buckley, M. Ronald, Diane C. Kicza, and Nancy Crane. 1987. "A Note on the Effectiveness of Flextime as an Organizational Intervention." *Public Personnel Journal* (Fall): 259–267.

Burns, Lawton. 1989. "Matrix Management in Hospitals: Testing Theories of Structure and Development." *Administrative Science Quarterly* (Sept): 349–368.

Burns, Tom, and G. M. Stalker. 1961. *The Management of Innovation.* London: Tavistock Institute.

Campion, Michael. 1988. "Interdisciplinary Approaches to Job Design: A Constructive Replication with Extensions." *Journal of Applied Psychology* (Aug): 467–481.

Chandler, Alfred D., Jr. 1962. *Strategy and Structure.* Cambridge, MA: MIT Press.

Cleland, David I., ed. 1984. *Matrix Management Systems Handbook.* New York: Van Nostrand Reinhold.

Drucker, Peter. 1988. "The Coming of the New Organization." *Harvard Business Review* 66: 45–53.

Hackman, J. R. and G. R. Oldham. 1980. *Work Redesign.* (Jan/Feb) Reading, MA: Addison-Wesley.

Lawrence, Paul, and Jay Lorsch. 1967. *Organization and Environment: Managing Differentiation and Integration.* Homewood, IL: Irwin.

Mintzberg, Henry. 1983. *Structure in Fives: Designing Effective Organizations.* Englewood Cliffs, NJ: Prentice Hall.

Shirley, Steve. 1986. "A Company Without Offices." *Harvard Business Review* 11: 127–136.

Smith, Adam. 1937. *Wealth of Nations.* New York: Modern Library; originally published in 1776.

Van Fleet, David, and Arthur G. Bedeian. 1977. "A History of the Span of Management." *Academy of Management Review* 2: 356–372.

Woodward, Joan. 1965. *Industrial Organization.* London: Oxford University Press.

11

Organizing Authority Relationships: Delegation

*O*nce the structural elements of an organization have been set, another organizing step remains. In order to obtain the synergy that results when people work together, the differentiated jobs and departments and spans of control require reintegration.

When the coordination aspects of organizing are weak, excessive conflict, neglected responsibilities, and poor control are typical symptoms.

When coordination is achieved, according to pioneering business philosopher Mary Parker Follett's 1924 book, Creative Experience, "you have a business with all its parts so coordinated, so moving together in their closely knit and adjusting activities, so linking, interlocking, interrelating, that they make a working unit." In this chapter, management functions that lead to smooth coordination are addressed.

AUTHORITY, POWER, AND INFLUENCE

Authority, power, and influence are key concepts in understanding how managers regulate and coordinate the activities of individuals and departments. All three relate in some way to a manager's right or ability to control others.

Authority

Authority is the right to influence others based on position. It is sometimes referred to as position power. In answer to the question, "What gives you the right to tell me what to do?" a person with authority would reply, "My position in the organization." Some organizations officially delegate a great deal of authority to all hierarchical levels. Other organizations keep most of the authority closely held in a few positions. The degree of delegated authority is one of the organizational design issues that will be discussed later in the chapter.

There are two major views about where the original authority arose: the classical view and the acceptance view. Each view has important implications for managers.

THE CLASSICAL VIEW

The classical view holds that authority originates at the very top of a society. In different societies, the very top might be God, the king or president, or the collective will of the people (a constitution). Authority is then legally delegated downward. For example, in the U.S. the Constitution grants the right to own and use private property to owners. The owners grant the Board of Directors authority to oversee the property. The Board grants authority to the company president who grants it to top managers who grant it to middle managers who grant it to supervisors.

The result of this view is that management has a legal right to give orders and subordinates have an obligation to obey. Managers who subscribe to this view tend to be autocratic in their directives. They take a "my way or the highway" tone with their subordinates, because they believe they have an absolute right to direct, based on their position in the organization.

THE ACCEPTANCE VIEW

The acceptance view of authority argues that authority exists only when the subordinate agrees that it does—only when the subordinate accepts the directives of the manager. This view developed from the observation that not all directives are obeyed. Some are accepted by the receiver and some are not. In the acceptance view, whether or not authority is present in any particular law or order is determined by the receiver, not the person issuing the order.

If a general tells the troops to "take the hill" and they just stand there, the number of stars on the collar is irrelevant, as some generals found out in Vietnam.

Of course, most directives given by managers are followed by their subordinates. Chester Barnard, in his 1938 book, *Functions of the Executive*, set out the conditions under which a subordinate will comply with managerial directives.

"A person can and will accept a communication as authoritative only when four conditions simultaneously obtain: (a) he can and does understand the communication; (b) *at the time of his decision* he believes that it is not inconsistent with the purpose of the organization; (c) *at the time of his decision* he believes it to be compatible with his personal interest as a whole; and (d) he is able mentally and physically to comply with it."

In addition to these conditions, authority is most likely to be accepted when the orders or directives fall within a familiar range of responsibility or activity. This range is called the "Zone of Indifference" or "area of acceptance." When a manager requests that a subordinate prepare an annual performance review, the subordinate will probably comply. On the other hand, should the manager request that the subordinate vote for a particular Senate candidate, the subordinate will most likely find the directive to be outside the area of acceptance.

A manager who assumes that the acceptance view of authority is true will use a more participative, consultive style of directing.

Power

While authority might be defined as the *right* to direct others, power can be defined as the *ability* to do so. The two abilities do not always go together. As the acceptance view of authority demonstrates, a person with the organizational right to command is not always followed. Alternatively, a person with power may have no legitimate right to direct, but may be very effective at it nonetheless.

This observation led John French and Bertram Raven to identify five sources of power. Each may occur at all levels of an organization.

LEGITIMATE POWER

Legitimate power is the power that goes along with an official position. When authority is defined as having the power of position, that is the same as saying it has legitimate power. Within certain bounds, the rights to exert influence associated with a person's job or position may be downward in the organization or upward. For example, the security guard has the legitimate power to ask every person who enters the factory to show his or her badge, including the president of the company.

REWARD POWER

Reward power is based on a person's ability to reward another. In an organization, typically some reward power goes along with the managerial position. However, people with no official position can provide rewards for certain behavior. For example, the captain of the company softball team can offer a place on the team roster to a worker who supplied helpful information. A secretary can reward a co-worker by completing a typing project ahead of others.

COERCIVE POWER

When someone has the ability to punish another, he or she has coercive power. Punishment may range from the loss of a minor privilege to the loss of a job. Coercion can be quite subtle and still be an effective influencer of behavior. Coercive power usually attends a managerial position, but, as with reward power, organizational members without legitimate authority may also have coercive power. For example, a secretary can punish a co-worker by placing his or her typing project behind others. Workers use coercive power to control management when they slow production by following their job descriptions to the letter.

EXPERT POWER

Expert power is the power someone has as the result of having specialized knowledge which someone else wants to know. In Alvin Toffler's 1990 book, *Power Shift*, and in Naisbitt and Aberdene's 1991 book, *Megatrends 2000*, the power of knowledge is highlighted as the greatest possible power, especially in the years ahead.

In the best of situations, managers have expert power in addition to their legitimate power. That is not always the case, however, especially in high-technology fields. For example, a university education in engineering is said to be good for five to seven years. After that, retraining is required to get engineers back up-to-date in their fields. As a result, research engineers may take their concerns to the most knowledgeable of their co-workers rather than take them to the boss.

REFERENT POWER

Referent power is also called charisma. It is the power that results because the person being influenced wants to identify with or imitate the influencer. Referent power depends on an individual's style and personality. John F. Kennedy and Ronald Reagan added referent power to the legitimate power of the Presidency.

Influence

Influence includes all the actions and examples that directly or indirectly cause a change in another's behavior or attitudes. Both authority and power may be used to exert influence. If a manager leaves work each day five to ten minutes before quitting time, she will, by example, influence others to leave work early. If a manager gives employees who have not missed a day of work a year-end bonus, he is using reward power to influence worker behavior.

Power in Organizations

The constructive use of power in organizations is an important coordinating element. David McClelland has described two faces of power. The negative side of power is expressed in dominance-submission terms. It means "power over" others. Leadership based on the negative face of power treats people as pawns in a game whose outcome is "I win; you lose." A manager exerting this kind of power might require subordinates to submit written requests for ordinary office supplies. The ultimate consequences of this type of power are subordinates who withdraw or who fight. Neither response is helpful in creating organizational synergy.

Power used positively can be thought of as "power with" others. It involves exerting influence on behalf of others rather than over them. The manager works with subordinates to garner necessary resources and overcome obstacles. For example, a manager exerting this type of power might work with human resources in order to get additional training for subordinates.

John Kotter has given the topic of power in organizations significant analysis. He has identified several key characteristics that are typical of managers who use power well.

1. They understand that power is necessary in the accomplishment of goals. They feel comfortable using power.

2. They appreciate that each of the five bases of power has merit. As a result, they try to develop strength in each.

3. They also understand that each power base has different costs and benefits, and so try to use the appropriate kind of power for a particular situation. For example, they do not use expert power outside of their own area of expertise. They do not use coercive power when reward power will work better.

4. They seek the use of power and build others' dependence on them. However, they understand the need to act maturely and avoid displays of power.

CENTRALIZATION AND DECENTRALIZATION

Because authority is tied to position or a particular job, jobs can be designed to include a great deal of authority or very little authority. When the owner and top managers of an organization keep most of the decision-making authority for themselves, the organization is said to be centralized. When the authority to make decisions, to hire and fire, to offer rewards or punishment is widely distributed to the different jobs, the organization is decentralized.

Because degree of decentralization is one of the elements of organization design and structure, the same factors that influence strategy, job design, and departmentation influence the appropriate amount of delegation of authority.

Size and Rate of Growth

The larger an organization becomes, the more delegation of authority must occur simply to handle the number and complexity of decisions that must be made. However, when the rate of growth slows, the organization may slowly work toward more centralization through narrower policies, procedures, and rules.

Strategy

The more a company relies on research and development and product innovation, the more it will tend toward decentralization. Because the expert skills are at the bottom of the organization, authority is widely distributed to all organizational members. On the other hand, companies in stable environments with consistent products tend toward centralization.

External Organizational Characteristics

On the average, workers today have more educational background than workers of the last generation. They also have greater expectations that work will make an important contribution to the quality of their lives. They want to take greater control of what they do and how they do it. These qualities of workers contribute to a trend toward greater decentralization.

Decentralization is also more efficient. If employees at all levels take on more decision-making authority, fewer expensive managers are needed to coordinate organizational activities.

Internal Organizational Characteristics

The skills of the managers and other internal characteristics influence how decentralized an organization can be and still reach its objectives. Some of the most important characteristics follow:

1. Managerial skills, especially of lower-level managers, must be strong enough to handle the authority. On the other hand, the organization must be willing to place trust in its employees and offer them the space to try and to learn from occasional failures.

2. Some decisions are too important or risky to delegate. In such cases, an organization will do better to remain centralized.

3. Organizational culture and traditions have a significant influence on whether or not an organization decentralizes. Some entire industries tend toward centralization, for example banking. Other industries share a culture of decentralized authority, for example computer software development. If a company started out with a very participa-

tive owner, it will likely remain more decentralized while an organization that began with a strong-willed leader will likely remain more centralized as it grows.

DELEGATION PROBLEMS

Even when an organization establishes a structure that supports decentralized decision making, some managers will resist accepting authority or delegating it to others. Authority implies responsibility. When a person assumes power or authority, he or she also assumes responsibility.

Authority and Responsibility

An interesting relationship exists between authority and responsibility. In order to meet responsibilities, employees need authority. If Max is given responsibility for keeping the small tools in order and accounted for, but he does not have the authority to lock them up, he will find his job impossible to perform. Authority must be delegated commensurate with responsibility.

However, no matter how much of a manager's job is delegated to others, the manager retains complete responsibility for seeing that the job is completed. Managers assign tasks and grant authority to subordinates. They customarily hold subordinates responsible for the results. But in doing so, they do not relieve themselves of responsibility. Instead, they extend the chain of responsibility to include another organizational level.

Not surprisingly, many people find it difficult to give the authority for a task to someone else if they remain responsible for it. This is one reason why some people avoid delegation. Delegation on an individual level and decentralization on an organizational level mean loss of control.

Lack of Organization

Managers will find it impossible to delegate effectively if they have not done thoughtful planning. Delegation requires flexibility and enough lead time to assign work, train where necessary, and establish a follow-up or feedback system.

Subordinate Insecurity

Sometimes organizations remain centralized because subordinates avoid taking on responsibility. As a risk-avoidance behavior, they want their bosses to make all the decisions. When subordinates fear criticism or dismissal for mistakes, they are even more reluctant to accept delegation.

In spite of all these reasons for avoiding delegation, managers must delegate and must teach their subordinates to accept delegated responsibility. If one person could do all the work, groups and organizations would not be necessary. As the time management section of chapter 9 discussed, tasks that are urgent but not important can be the first ones to be delegated.

STAFF VS. LINE AUTHORITY

Authority has been defined as the legitimate right to direct the activities of others. Many organizations have fine-tuned that definition, dividing authority into two kinds: line authority and staff authority.

Line Authority

Organizations have objectives. "Line" managers are those managers who are directly responsible for achieving those objectives. For example, in a manufacturing plant, the supervisor of the assembly department is a line manager. So is the plant manager and the CEO. However, the accounting department manager is not a line manager and does not have line authority. On the other hand, an accountant working for Arthur Anderson Accountancy company does hold a line position, because the organizational objectives will be directly affected by an accountant's work.

Staff Authority

All those managers in departments and functions that support the line are called "staff." In the manufacturing plant example, the accounting department manager holds a staff position and has staff authority. Staff employees provide line managers with advice and service.

The reason for the distinction is that in many cases line authority carries with it the legitimate right to direct the activities of staff personnel. However, rarely does staff authority carry with it the right to direct line personnel. This difference can and does lead to friction. Staff employees resist being directed by someone other than their bosses, while line personnel believe staff personnel exist only to serve them. Many organizations are trying to reduce the focus on staff and line differences, saying instead that all employees are necessary to the achievement of organizational objectives.

Both differentiation and integration are important to effective organizational design. How an organization handles the broad topic of authority relationships is key to good integration of activities.

Authority is a concept that applies at the organizational level; power is the related individual-level concept. Decentralization is an organizational concept; delegation is the same concept on an individual level. These four processes provide a significant part of the coordination important to good organizational design.

Selected Readings

Barnard, Chester I. 1938. *Functions of the Executive.* Cambridge, MA: Harvard University Press.

Burns, Tom, and G. M. Stalker. 1961. *The Management of Innovation.* London: Tavistock Institute.

French, John R. P., and Bertram Raven. 1959. "The Bases of Social Power." *Studies in Social Power* edited by Dorwin Cartwright. Ann Arbor: University of Michigan Press.

Gibson, James L., John M. Ivancevich, and James H. Donnelly, Jr. 1988. *Organizations: Behavior, Structure, Processes*, 6th ed. Plano, TX: Business Publications.

Gooding, R. Z., and J. A. Wagner III. 1985. "A Meta-Analytic Review of the Relationship Between Size and Performance: The Productivity and Efficiency of Organizations and Their Subunits." *Administrative Science Quarterly* (Dec): 462–481.

Lawrence, Raul R., and Jay W. Lorsch. 1967. *Organization and Environment: Managing Differentiation and Integration*. Homewood, IL: Irwin.

MacMillan, Ian C., and Patricia E. Jones. 1984. "Designing Organizations to Compete." *Journal of Business Strategy* (Spring): 22–26.

Nossiter, Vivian. 1979. "A New Approach Toward Resolving the Line and Staff Dilemma." *Academy of Management Review* 4: 103–106.

Pfeffer, Jeffrey. 1981. *Power in Organizations*. Marshfield, MA: Pitman Publishing.

Robbins, Stephen P. 1990. *Organization Theory: Structure, Design, and Applications*, 3rd ed. Englewood Cliffs, NJ: Prentice–Hall.

VanFleet, David D. 1983. "Span of Management Research and Issues." *Academy of Management Review* 8: 546–552.

Weber, Max. 1953 (originally 1925). "The Three Types of Managerial Rule." *Berkeley Journal of Sociology*,4: 1–11.

12

Managing the Informal Organization: Conflict and Stress

*O*rganizational design establishes the formal structure of an organization—the jobs people perform, the kinds of departments they work in, the authority relationships among them, and the number each manager supervises. In addition to this formal structure, every organization has an informal structure, a network of relationships which overlaps the formal structure.

The relationships in the informal organization can add significant energy to the formal organization, helping it achieve its objectives. Alternatively, the informal organization can cause conflict and stress, reducing personal and organizational effectiveness.

Every organization has an informal sub-organization. Nothing a manager can do will change that. However, managers can take steps which will increase the positive consequences of the informal network, while reducing stress and conflict. This chapter discusses conflict and stress in organizations.

THE INFORMAL ORGANIZATION

The informal organization consists of groupings or relationships among organizational members which may be more influential than the formal relationships established by the organization's structure. The informal organization arises when people share interests or work closely together on projects. For example, four employees who carpool may be very close friends, each looking out for promotion opportunities or listening for information about budgets and schedules to share with the others. However, at work they may be in different departments or even different buildings.

Advantages of the Informal Organization

Informal groups perform important functions for the organization as a whole. They establish and reinforce the behaviors and values important to the group, they stimulate communication, and they provide socializing opportunities.

Because of their largely emotional nature, informal groups provide energy, innovation, and vitality to the organization. Because the membership of various informal groups is different from the membership of formal groups, a tight web of interlinking, overlapping relationships exist in any organization. Information can be communicated rapidly through an organization as a result. If a secretary in the purchasing department hears that four new sets of office furniture have been ordered, within hours many in the organization will be speculating on what that means—new hires, refurbishing, new promotions? When the information is perceived to be critical to employees, perhaps knowledge about raises or layoffs, the informal communication network can work in minutes. (This topic is addressed more fully in chapter 18 on communication.)

Disadvantages of the Informal Organization

Informal groups are like formal groups in that they develop group goals. Sometimes the two sets of goals are counter to each other. For example, the standard production rate might be seven to ten units per hour; however, the informal understanding among the workers is exactly seven units per hour, never more. Even when informal values and behavior encourage a group to do more than expected, conflict and stress can result. As the next section will detail, managers can manage at least some of the factors which lead to conflict.

CONFLICT

Organizational conflict is disagreement between or among organizational members which arises because they must share scarce resources or engage in interdependent activities when they have different values, goals, perceptions, or status. In other words, conflict is inevitable. Fortunately, conflict can be managed such that the outcomes are positive ones.

Traditional View of Conflict

Classical management theorists like Frederick Taylor believed that conflict was a sure sign of poor management. They believed any energy an employee spent on conflict with another employee was lost productivity. All conflict was seen as dysfunctional.

Current View of Conflict

The current thinking on conflict, called the *interactionist view* by management author Stephen Robbins, is that conflict is not only inevitable, it is necessary for generating creative, innovative solutions to problems. Indeed, a great deal of conflict is dysfunctional; but when managed, conflict can increase organizational effectiveness. When conflict is too low, the organization will change too slowly to keep up with environmental changes. When conflict is too high, it distracts organizational members from meeting their objectives.

Causes of Conflict

A more specific understanding of the conditions that encourage conflict will help in managing it. The individuals involved, as well as their managers, can benefit from thinking about what contributes to conflict.

CONFLICTING OBJECTIVES

If one member of a family wants to vacation at the beach and another wants to see Mount Rushmore, the family has a conflict of objectives. At work, if the production department has a units-per-day objective and the quality control department has a product quality objective, the organization has a conflict of objectives. Any time the achievement of one person's objectives interferes with the achievement of another person's objectives, conflict will arise. In the chapters on planning, the importance of developing goals that support each other was discussed. Conflict is one outcome of poor planning.

SCARCE RESOURCES

Money, equipment, and space are always in short supply. When two or more people believe they have the greater right to limited resources, conflict results. A new copy machine in the purchasing department can cause bitterness in the payroll department. Labor and management are traditionally in conflict over who has the greater right to the profits.

PERSONALITY

Just the fact that people have different ways of being in the world can result in interpersonal conflict. A nonsmoker may mount a campaign against the two smokers in the office. Two highly competitive workers may end up in frequent conflict. Some people have high control needs. When two people, each wanting to control, must work together, conflict is likely.

PERCEPTION

Each person has a perceptual set—a tendency to interpret information in a certain recurring way. Some people see the opportunity in every situation; others consistently see the threat. Several factors influence people's perceptual sets: their different sensory abilities (some people hear better, some people taste a greater variety of tastes); their childhoods (some people were well loved, some were not); their cultures (some believe it is important to save the old, some believe it is important to build new). Life experiences also contribute to the meaning people attribute to things. A person who is anxious about losing her job is likely to become very tense when her boss walks into her office. On the other hand, an employee who has just concluded a major sale will be very pleased to see his boss walk into his office.

Conflict can be created when individuals reach widely different conclusions based on their different perceptual sets or experiences.

INTERDEPENDENT WORK ACTIVITIES

When two or more subunits depend on each other to complete their respective tasks, conflict (or cooperation) may arise. Organizations with multiple shifts frequently experience intershift conflict; each shift is dependent on what the previous shift accomplished, whether or not they maintained the equipment, and if they restocked supplies.

At one assembly plant, day-shift employees believed night-shift employees deliberately broke equipment at the end of their shift so day-shift productivity would be down and night-shift productivity would appear better. Of course, the day-shift's response was to retaliate, and conditions got worse before they got better.

ORGANIZATIONAL AMBIGUITIES

Sometimes the organization causes conflict because it fails to make goals and work responsibilities clear. When each of three managers thinks someone else is responsible for preparing end-of-year reports, conflict will arise. If Fred believes he has the authority to assign work to Jeff, but Jeff believes he need only respond to work assigned by Anne, conflict between Fred and Jeff is certain to result.

POOR COMMUNICATION

An amazing amount of conflict arises as the result of poor communication. When people misunderstand each other, they are more likely to find themselves in conflict. If a subordinate does not understand an assignment, yet fails to say so, a conflict can be expected when the work is not completed as the boss anticipates. Although humans spend most of their waking time in communication behaviors, they are not necessarily good communicators. All communication skills must be learned and then practiced. (Chapter 18 offers some communication skill-building ideas.)

CHANGE

Most people resist change. The unknown is scary. As a result, the few who want change are certain to find themselves in conflict with those who do not. Because organizations must change frequently to remain competitive, and because dysfunctional conflict is a likely result of change, managing change is a major managerial concern. Chapter 24 addresses this topic in fuller detail.

Managing Conflict

Different people take different approaches to handling the conflict in their lives. Although a person may use different approaches in different situations, most people come to rely on a certain response mode. All conflict resolution approaches have some benefit to the user; however, the problem-solving approach is far superior to other approaches in its long-run effectiveness.

A person's overall, or usual, conflict resolution style is a significant contributor to his or her management style. In chapter 6, decision-making was identified as the "core" management function. The need for decision making is frequently the result of conflict having arisen somewhere in the manager's area of authority. When conflict arises, a manager must make a decision. So conflict resolution style becomes the measure of the manager.

FORCING

One way to resolve conflict is to use power—to force the other person into accepting a decision. When this approach to conflict resolution is used, one person wins and the other loses. In the short run, forcing "works." The conflict is resolved, usually in very little time. As a management style, forcing is called "autocratic."

However, the long-run costs of overpowering the other party can be extreme. Resentment builds in the loser and sabotage may be the result.

Examples abound. In war, the weaker party talks about losing the battle but not the war and uses underground tactics. At work, managers who use an autocratic style frequently experience high turnover among their employees and costly equipment breakdown problems.

AVOIDING

Some people avoid conflict—they flee from it. As a first step, they might ignore the problem and pretend that the conflict does not exist. If the situation becomes too uncomfortable to ignore, the avoider will leave, either actually or figuratively. The result is that those in conflict are essentially unmanaged—they have no guidance or leadership. The solutions that result from such a situation are likely to be less than ideal. As a management style, this is called laissez-faire, which means "to let (people) do (as they choose)" in French.

Some withdrawing managers schedule out-of-town business meetings when conflict gets too much for them to ignore. Telling subordinates their conflict has nothing to do with the manager and, therefore, they should resolve it is another response in this conflict resolution approach.

SMOOTHING

Some people avoid conflict by giving in. Rather than deal with the interpersonal friction, they smooth things over. Getting along is more important than any substantive issue for this type of conflict resolver. In terms of management style, this approach is called "country club management."

Giving in is absolutely appropriate when the party to a conflict is in error, or when the matter is a minor one. However, the manager who habitually gives in is easily controlled by others. The organization loses when conflict is hidden or smoothed over.

COMPROMISING

To compromise means to settle by concession. In a compromise, all parties to a conflict give up something. Compromise, as a conflict resolution approach, has traditionally been highly valued in the U.S. Parents admonish their children to "share" and "take turns." The labor union seeks an 8 percent raise; management offers a 4 percent raise; they compromise at 6 percent.

The compromise approach to conflict resolution is typical of the "bureaucratic" or political management style. In many cases, compromise is perceived as the most "fair" way to resolve conflict—everyone gets something.

The problem with compromise is that everyone also loses something. Suppose a company has $70,000 for capital equipment purchases this year. One department requests $60,000 to buy a processing machine and another requests $40,000 to change outdated fixtures. If the manager takes a 50-50 compromise approach to this conflict over scarce resources, each department would get $35,000—not enough for either to make a productive purchase. Compromise frequently results in no winners.

PROBLEM SOLVING

The problem-solving approach to conflict encourages the parties involved to look for innovative solutions where everyone is a winner. Typically, "stepping back" so the perspective changes allows people to see more. In the resource allocation problem above, taking an 18-month perspective might allow both departments to meet their needs. Perhaps one of the departments is not really "ready" to make the purchase, even if it were funded, and waiting 18 months would give them an opportunity to thoroughly research the equipment options.

Considering management styles, the problem-solving approach is typical of the "participative" manager. High trust and good interpersonal communication are required to make problem solving work.

MEDIATION/ARBITRATION

If the parties to a conflict are too entrenched in their own positions to gain a broader perspective, it may be helpful to use an outside neutral party to assist in the conflict resolution. Mediators listen to each side and recommend a solution. Arbitrators develop a solution which each side agrees beforehand will be binding. Frequently, union-management conflicts are settled through arbitration. Many physicians ask their patients to agree to arbitration rather than lawsuits if they have a conflict over the quality of their medical care.

SUPERORDINATE GOALS

Some conflict situations can be resolved because the individuals involved are willing to set aside their own interests in order to meet some larger, shared goal. For example, labor and management at Chrysler may experience many conflicts during good economic times. However, when the firm was facing bankruptcy, the larger shared goal of survival got the two sides working together.

ENGINEERED CONFLICT SOLUTIONS

Frequently, interpersonal conflicts can be solved by changing the structure rather than by trying to change the people involved. If two workers are having personality clashes, moving them to different offices will most likely help. Layout of the physical plant can encourage or discourage interaction. Clarifying job descriptions and reporting relationships can help reduce conflict. Especially in situations where the manager tends to withdraw from conflict, more narrowly defined procedures and rules can keep things running smoothly.

Conflict distracts from the work at hand. However, when it is managed well, it can lead to innovation, creativity, and excitement. When conflict is mismanaged, it becomes dysfunctional. The system can become consumed by anger, bitterness, and sabotage. Dysfunctional conflict leads to stress.

THE STRESS RESPONSE

Stress is the body's physiological and psychological response to demands made on it. The demands can be environmental—noise, dust, smoke, job monotony, physical exhaustion—or psychological—a promotion, a friend's death, being fired, or graduating from school. If a stress response is triggered, it does not matter if the stress is caused by a positive experience or a negative one. A wedding can cause stress just as a divorce can. A promotion can be as stressful as losing a job.

When the body is stressed, it releases certain hormones which first cause "positive" stress. The blood pressure to the brain is increased and the blood pressure to the hands and feet is decreased. This level of physiological response allows a person to think more clearly. It also explains why a person's hands are likely to be cold during a job interview.

The second stage in a stress response prepares the body for fight or flight. The blood pressure falls in the brain and goes up in the large muscles of the arms and legs. During this level of stress, people can run very fast or lift very heavy weights. Bar room brawls are most likely to occur at this level of stress. In an organization, fighting or fleeing are typically inappropriate. When the body is prepared for an action it cannot take, toxins build up in the muscle tissue. Eventually the toxic by-products of stress lead to disease. Colds, flu, and sinus infections are as symptomatic of stress as cancer and heart attacks.

The third level of stress is called "shock" or "exhaustion" depending on how rapidly it occurs. If this level of stress is the result of an accident, it is referred to as shock. If the body reaches this level of stress as the result of a slow accumulation of toxins, it is called exhaustion. When exhaustion occurs as the result of work issues, it is called burnout. During this level of stress, the blood pressure falls throughout the body. If blood pressure to the brain remains too low too long, death results.

When Hans Selye first defined stress in the 1930s, he and other researchers believed that moderate stress levels were beneficial, resulting in greater individual productivity. Too much stress and too little stress were both seen as counterproductive. Current medical research has reached a different conclusion. First, the definition of stress has been changed somewhat. Events do not cause stress. Stress is the mind-body response to events. In other words, the stressor is what the person thinks or feels about the event, not the event itself. Running out of gas is not of itself stressful. *Thinking* about being late to work, having to walk along a busy road, and getting dirty are what make the event stressful. Some young lovers have found running out of gas to be very pleasant because their thoughts were focused on how much time they would get to spend together as a result!

The second current finding about stress is that each person appears to have a fixed ability to handle stress. When that amount of stress has been experienced, the person dies. At least 70 percent of all illness has been proven to be the result of stress. Based on these findings, stress avoidance is life enhancing.

Stress in Organizations

Organizations are increasingly interested in the topic of stress for two reasons. First, stress-induced illness results in lost worker productivity. Second, the courts are finding organizations liable for the stress their employees are experiencing.

Organizations are working to offer programs that help counteract the negative consequences of stress. Job design that allows greater worker autonomy, membership in health clubs, quiet rooms for employee breaks, better job training, and "work buddy" or mentoring programs are helping. Employee assistance programs that offer confidential legal, drug, alcohol, and psychiatric counseling are gaining popularity.

Conflict and stress are discussed together in this chapter, because conflict is stressful for many people. Because their experience with conflict has taught them that they are likely to lose something, their minds respond with fearful, stress-inducing thoughts as conflict builds around them. As a result, learning to solve conflicts with win-win solutions is an important, organizationwide managerial stress-reduction tool.

Managers and Stress

In addition to organizationwide programs, individual managers can make a difference in the stress their employees experience. According to legend, "Typhoid Annie" spread typhoid as she served food in a restaurant. She herself never experienced the disease, but she was a carrier. Some managers are "Stress Annies." By constantly changing the rules, communicating job assignments poorly, and fostering rather than solving conflict, managers can add to their subordinates' stress levels.

Alternatively, managers can reduce subordinates' stress levels by developing attainable objectives, delegating authority with responsibility, developing trust, and communicating clearly.

*I*n addition to an organization's formal structure there is an entire network of informal relationships which cross departments and levels. These interpersonal relationships create the emotional energy which sustains the organizational system.

These relationships can also create conflict and stress. Part of a manager's job is seeing that the tasks get done and the objectives are met. Part of a manager's job is seeing that the relationships among coworkers are maintained, that conflict does not become dysfunctional, and that employee stress levels remain healthfully low.

Selected Readings

Baron, R. A. 1984."Reducing Organizational Conflict: An Incompatible Response Approach."*Journal of Applied Psychology* 69: 272–279.

Brief, A. P., R. S. Schuler, and M. Van Sell. 1981. *Managing Job Stress.* Boston: Little, Brown.

Fisher, R., and W. Urey. 1981. *Getting to Yes: Negotiating Agreement Without Giving In.* Boston: Houghton Mifflin Company.

Freudenberger, H. J. 1980. *Burnout: The High Cost of High Achievement.* Garden City, NY: Anchor Press.

Gabarro, J., and J. Kotter. 1980. "Managing Your Boss." *Harvard Business Review* 58: 92–100.

Ganster, D. C., M. R. Fusilier, and B. T. Mayes. 1986. "Role of Social Support in the Experience of Stress at Work." *Journal of Applied Psychology* 71: 102–110.

Ivancevich, J. M., M. T. Matteson, and E. P. Richards III. 1985. "Who's Liable for Stress on the Job?" *Harvard Business Review* 63: 60.

Levinson, H. 1981. "When Executives Burn Out." *Harvard Business Review* 59: 75–78.

Morley, D. D., and P. Schockley-Zalabak. 1986. "Conflict Avoiders and Compromisers: Toward an Understanding of Their Organizational Communication Style." *Group and Organization Studies* 11: 387–402.

Quick, J. C., and J. D. Quick. 1990. *Organizational Stress and Preventive Management.* 2nd ed. New York: McGraw-Hill.

Rubin, J. Z. 1983. "Negotiation." *American Behavioral Scientist* 27: 136–148.

Selye, H. 1976. *The Stress of Life*, 2nd ed. New York: McGraw-Hill.

Spector, P. E., D. J. Dwyer, and S. M. Jex. 1988. "Relation of Job Stressors to Affective, Health, and Performance Outcomes: A Comparison of Multiple Data Sources." *Journal of Applied Psychology* 73: 11–19.

13

Human Resource Management

Part of developing the structure of an organization is designing jobs. Human Resource Management (HRM) is the function of management concerned with finding the right people to fill those jobs—with staffing the organization.

Since the composition of an organization's workforce is constantly changing, the process of staffing is ongoing. And since the most important resource most organizations have is their workforce, the quality of the work the staffing function performs is vital to organizational success.

In addition to finding the right people for each position, the HRM function includes training them in the culture of the organization as well as in specific job skills, developing employees to get them ready for promotion, and evaluating their performance.

HUMAN RESOURCE MANAGEMENT

Human Resource Management might be defined as finding the right person with the right skills in the right place at the right time with the right motivation to accomplish strategic objectives. The importance of this goal makes the topic of staffing important to every manager. A common complaint, especially of small business owners, is that they "can't get good people."

The staffing function requires managers to have a great deal of specialized knowledge. Large organizations are likely to have an entire HRM department, with experts in each of the subspecialities. Because they realize the importance and difficulty of the staffing function, they are willing to invest significant resources in it.

The major tasks that fall under the staffing function are human resource planning, recruiting, selecting, orienting, training, developing, and appraising. Related to these tasks are decruitment—when the company downsizes—and establishing pay/benefits packages.

HUMAN RESOURCE PLANNING

The first step in thoughtful HRM is establishing the organization's need for labor, not just today, but in the future. This step is called human resource planning. Human resource planning, like planning in general, requires forecasts of projected supply and projected demand.

Forecasting Resource Supply

In forecasting the potential supply of labor, several factors need to be considered. One source of forecasting data is called demographics—the study of population dynamics. Since even entry-level workers are at least sixteen or seventeen years old when they begin work, demographers already know a great deal about the workforce of the year 2000. The very youngest of them are now seven. Most of them are considerably older. Demographers know how much schooling they will have and what they are studying in school, as well as where they live and what their ethnic background is. On the following page is a table (Fig. 13.1) containing information about the workforce and how it is changing.

The data suggest a workforce that is older, has more women and ethnic minorities, includes more people from households where both parents work and from single-parent households, and is better educated than the workforce of ten years earlier. These changes will influence how the workforce needs to be managed.

Forecasting Resource Demand

In forecasting organizational demand for workers, human resource managers consider the skills required first. Given the job descriptions of unfilled positions, what qualities are required? This step is called *job analysis*.

Work Group	1964	1984	1995 (est)
	Percent Working		
Men	83	77	76
Women	38	55	60
Mothers	32	60	67
With High School Education	45	60	61
With College Education	11	21	23

Occupation	Percent of All Workers		
White Collar	37	43	46
Blue Collar	37	29	29
Service/Sales	19	26	23
Farming/Fishing	8	3	2
Median Age of Workforce	(n.a.)	35.2	37.6

Population Dynamics: Age	1980	1985	1990
	In Thousands		
16–24	25,453	24,254	22,139
25–54	63,396	71,515	79,466
65 and over	3,007	3,017	3,102

Fig. 13.1 Changes in Workforce

ASSESSING CURRENT NEED

Assessing current need means calculating the number and kind of positions that are currently unfilled. "Current" usually means within the next year; if the company is aware that William will be retiring in June, his replacement would be considered current.

ASSESSING FUTURE DEMAND

Different industries and job categories have different turnover rates. The *turnover rate* is the percent of workers who leave the job each year. They might leave for a variety of reasons—got a better job, retired, were fired. Several years ago, the turnover rate for retail employees at Target Stores was 100 percent! That means that by the end of the year, the number of new employees was equal to the total number of jobs. On the other hand, turnover among the staff at California State University, Chico has averaged less than seven percent over the last ten years. An organization must replace the employees it loses to turnover.

Planned growth or retrenchment will affect future need as well. When thinking about future demand, another consideration is timing. Some workers will need additional training and experience in order to be ready for promotions. Planning for promotions is called *succession planning*. Succession planning is often overlooked by organizations with the consequence that the organization lacks leadership when a manager leaves suddenly. Even very small organizations are improved by assessing future workforce needs. Tri-Counties Bank, a rapidly-growing regional bank, was nearly undone when two of the top six managers left within two months. The company had not considered succession planning. No one had been developed to take over in such a situation, and, as the rest of the chapter will detail, hiring qualified replacements from outside the company is a major project, rarely accomplished rapidly.

Identifying Resource Requirements

An official HRM plan lists the estimated shortages, in number and kind, and indicates areas of over-staffing. Frequently, the plan lists specific people by name and specifies the kinds of training they will need and the possible promotions that would give them the necessary experience. The plan gives an organization enough lead time to hire and train with care. Because of the sensitive nature of the information contained in an HRM plan, the information is confidential and limited to top managers.

RECRUITING AND SELECTING

Once the human resource needs are known, the process of recruiting and selecting can begin. Recruitment involves locating and attracting qualified candidates. Applicants can come from within the organization or from the outside. Once a pool of applicants for a position has been found, the right candidate for the job is selected.

Some companies have a traditional preference for promoting from within; some prefer outside candidates. When employees are hired from within, the sense is that good work will be rewarded and that "you can go places with this company." Morale is increased. When a job is advertised to current employees, it is called *job posting*. On the other hand, bringing in employees from outside introduces new ideas and new ways of doing things.

The goal of recruiting is to generate a large number of applicants for the job. A large hiring pool gives the organization the best opportunity to find the right worker for the job and the organization.

People who want to be considered for a position complete an application. Equal employment opportunity (EEO) laws, which will be discussed specifically later, require that the application form not ask for information about color, race, age, sex, national origin, veteran status, religion, and mental or physical handicaps.

The exception to this federal law is when a bonafide occupational qualification (BFOQ) exists. A *bonafide occupational qualification* is a qualification which limits the number of acceptable applicants based on, for example, age. In the United States, people under the age of 21 are not allowed to drink alcohol or serve it to others. As a result, an application form for a bar job may ask "Are you over 21?" It may not ask "How old are you?" Because there is a bias against them, older workers are protected under EEO laws from discrimination based on age.

Passive Recruiting

Some companies are passive recruiters. They do not advertise their positions but rather wait for applicants to walk in the door. Passive recruiting costs less, as long as the best job candidate is found. Some industries such as banking have such a steady rate of applications that more active recruitment is unnecessary.

Active Recruiting

Active recruiting means the organization actively seeks applicants. It might place want ads in newspapers, on radio, and in trade journals. The *Wall Street Journal* has a weekly job openings section. Several publications are exclusively job announcements—the *California Job Journal* and the *National Employment Weekly,* for example.

Many organizations send recruiters to college campuses and to job fairs. They visit high schools and send letters to people about to leave the military. They also use the services of employment agencies—for example, state departments of employment, headhunters, and professional agencies such as Dunhill. Unions frequently recruit workers for organizations.

Selection

Selection involves a number of screening steps. Research in the area of selection indicates that frequently each of these steps is a search for negative information. Rather than looking for the perfect candidate, what sometimes happens is a search for negative information—what is *wrong* with the candidate. In general, the selection process uses some or all of the following screening devices.

1. application form (or resume and application letter)

2. job skills testing

3. interviews

4. reference/recommendation checks

5. physical exam/drug testing

APPLICATION FORM

The information an applicant provides on the application is used to see if the applicant meets the minimum requirements for experience and education. The application can also provide information on a candidate's attention to detail and written communication skills.

JOB SKILLS TESTING

Some jobs require certain measurable skills. In those situations, skill testing is an effective way to screen applicants for ability. Typing/keyboarding tests, welding tests, and manual dexterity tests are typical.

Psychological Testing. Some companies use psychological or personality tests. For example, companies may look for indicators of extroversion in applicants for sales representative jobs. The Myers Briggs Personality Inventory is probably the most widely used of the personality tests because it has received the most validation research.

Test Validation. In order to use any screening test, the company must be able to demonstrate that people taking the test at different times score the same—*reliability*—and that the factor being tested for has job significance—*validity*. That is, does a high score correlate well with good job performance, and vice versa?

Assessment Centers. Especially when companies are selecting applicants for managerial positions, they might use a testing procedure conducted at an assessment center. The procedure is usually a two- or three-day group test with exercises designed to simulate actual managerial work. A large number of evaluators observe the performance of job candidates while they solve problems, write memos, conduct meetings, and give presentations. Assessment centers have proven very accurate at predicting managerial success.

INTERVIEWS

Over and over, the interview has been shown to be the weakest link in the selection process. The ability to talk with someone about a job is not the same as the ability to do it. In fact, if the interviewer is not trained, interview performance is not correlated with job performance at all. Personal bias about issues like appearance get in the way of thoughtful applicant screening. If an applicant's answer to a question is particularly thoughtful and demonstrates appropriate experience, but no other applicants were asked the same question, the interviewer does not have a comparable data base.

INTERVIEWER SKILLS

Interviewing skills can be learned which will markedly improve the reliability of interviewing as a screening device. The following guidelines will help managers do a more effective job of interviewing.

Plan for the Interview. Know the job description and the specific skills required to perform it well. Write out a list of questions. Phrase the question so they ask for more than facts and figures. Some examples might be: "Can you tell me of a specific example of a time when you had to make a decision under pressure," or "Describe for me the qualities of a specific person you have enjoyed working with." Check the list of questions to make sure they do not constitute discrimination and that they elicit information relevant to the specific job skills required. Read the job candidate's application/resume carefully and note any items that require clarification.

Create a Good Climate. Do not allow normal work to interrupt the interview. Moving to a quiet room with no phone might be best. Help the interviewee to relax, perhaps by talking about social topics first or making a positive comment about some element of the application.

Conduct a Goal-Directed Interview. Focus on the questions and job specifications and avoid the tendency to turn the interview into a casual conversation. Use the list of questions to provide similar structure to each interview. Provide interviewees with realistic information about the job and the company.

Make Written Notes. Immediately after the interview, evaluate the candidate's strengths and weaknesses for the position. Write down the evaluations for later comparison.

INTERVIEWEE SKILLS

Obviously the organization wants to find the best candidate for the job, but the applicant also wants the best possible person/job match. By developing good interviewee skills, applicants can improve the effectiveness of selection interviews as well. The following guidelines will help applicants with their role in the interviewing process.

Be Prepared. Research the potential employer. Large organizations are typically written about in the press; small organizations belong to local Chambers of Commerce or business associations. Public and university libraries carry reference materials on both local and national companies. Research the job being applied for. The Department of Labor publishes numerous dictionaries of jobs—also available at the library.

Consider the Nonverbal Cues. First impressions are very important in any interpersonal interaction. Arrive promptly. Dress appropriately for a person doing the job being applied for. Hair and clothes must be neat and clean. In the U. S., shake hands firmly and make direct eye contact.

Practice. Role playing—both interviewee and interviewer parts—with a friend is extremely helpful. Because interviewing is a skill, it can be learned. The best time to practice is before the first interview. Think up answers to questions likely to be asked.

Interview the Interviewer. Interviews are not one-way communications. The applicant needs information about the job and the company. Preparing questions ahead will result in better quality information. Sometimes companies paint a rosier picture of the job and its importance to the organization than is accurate. Careful questioning will assure more realistic information.

REFERENCE/RECOMMENDATIONS CHECK

Historically, the best information about the quality of an applicant's work was provided by his or her previous employers. In the last decade, however, individuals have been granted large awards in liability lawsuits against former employers who made negative comments without proof. For example, an employee of an industrial company was let go for stealing. The company did not press criminal charges. Because the employee was not accused and found guilty by a court of law, the company was libelous when it told a potential employer she had stolen from the company. Many organizations will now only verify the dates of employment.

PHYSICAL EXAMS

When the job requires that an employee perform physical labor, most companies require a physical exam. Examples are fire fighting and grocery clerking. Organizations want to be certain that they are not asking an employee to perform beyond his or her physical capacity.

A growing issue for organizations and employees alike is the use of drugs and alcohol at work. An increasing number of organizations are requiring drug tests as a condition of employment. The legality of drug testing is being questioned in the courts. The tests are not perfectly reliable; but more important, in terms of privacy issues, the tests pick up traces of drugs or alcohol used days or weeks before—perhaps while an employee was on vacation. The question becomes "when does the company's right to control worker behavior cease?"

ORIENTATION

Once the decision has been made to hire a particular individual, orientation begins. *Orientation* is a special subcategory of job training designed to introduce the employee to the organization. It might be called socializing because it teaches about the organization's culture and expected social behavior. Usually the same orientation training is given to all new employees, regardless of the job each will perform. New vice-presidents as well as new maintenance workers are taught about benefits, vacation time, company policies, and company history.

TRAINING AND DEVELOPMENT

Training assists an employee with learning specific job-related skills. *Development* focuses on the long-term growth of the employee, perhaps helping him or her to develop the perspective required for promotion. U. S. businesses are now spending over $30 billion per year on employee training and development. Companies expect to spend an average of about $100,000 on training each new employee over his or her first three years.

Because training and development are so expensive, more and more corporations are becoming partners with standard educational institutions. Hewlett-Packard provides several universities with engineering and computing equipment. As a result, graduates of the programs are more technically current. Apple Computer provides substantial educational discounts for all levels of school programs, with the result that computer literacy is increasingly developed in workers of the future. Pharmaceutical firms establish joint research and development projects with graduate medical programs.

Training

Training can be on-site, at the company, or it can be provided by consultants off-site.

ON-THE-JOB TRAINING

On-the-job training (OJT) means that the employee is actually performing the task during training. Although the majority of employees receive their training on the job, it is rarely the most efficient way to train. The person doing the training is disrupted from his or her own productivity. The trainee does not necessarily learn the best techniques, and some crucial steps may be overlooked completely, because the need for them did not naturally occur during the training.

VESTIBULE TRAINING

Vestibule training is handled in a special training facility where working conditions can be simulated and, at the same time, controlled. For example, Alpha Beta food stores has a grocery store "classroom" where new employees learn store layout, check-out procedures, and customer relations. McDonald's operates Hamburger University, where managers study all aspects of McDonald's fast-food service.

Development

Development is a long-term commitment to employees' personal development. Many companies will pay for books and tuition so employees can pursue formal education. Some companies even allow paid leave so employees can attend classes scheduled during working hours. Some companies support employees who want to volunteer for community service. Others pay workshop registration or certification exam fees.

The reasoning behind corporate support for personal development is that employees who are growing and learning new things bring creativity and innovation to the organization. They have a broader perspective and make more thoughtful decisions. As John F. Kennedy said, "Leadership and learning are indispensable to each other" (1963).

APPRAISAL

The human resource management function includes the task of developing employee appraisal systems. The appraisal system addresses questions like the following.

1. How frequently should employee performance be reviewed?
2. Who will review each employee?
3. To what degree will compensation be related to performance?
4. Who will establish performance standards?
5. What will happen if an employee fails to meet performance standards?

Some appraisal systems use standardized appraisal forms. Human resource managers are also responsible for developing review forms and testing them for applicability and reliability.

The most important issue in designing a formal appraisal system is that employee evaluation is linked to employee motivation. When an employee receives formal feedback of a negatively critical nature, performance tends to fall. Research indicates the following suggestions will promote healthy, motivating performance evaluation.

1. Manager and employee jointly set performance goals.
2. Manager provides ongoing informal feedback.
3. Manager and employee jointly review progress toward goals.
4. Corporate culture supports performance evaluation.
5. Newly hired employees receive clear information about how performance will be measured.
6. The relationship between pay and performance is clear.

7. The employee is an equal and active partner throughout the appraisal process.

HUMAN RESOURCE MANAGEMENT AND THE LAW

Managing the human resource is made especially difficult because of the legal technicalities that influence what an organization can do relative to its employees. Any society's economic system is central to the well-being of its citizens. As a result, all societies have a vested interest in controlling the action of the economy. Laws with far-reaching consequences are passed to control the citizen/organization interaction.

Occupational Health and Safety

Many jobs have the potential to harm the workers performing them. In response, in 1970, the federal government passed the Occupational Safety and Health Act (OSHA) which requires employers to provide a work environment free of recognized safety and health hazards. Some examples of the positive application of OSHA include ear protection for all workers in high noise areas, removal of asbestos from the working environment, dust removal systems in wood-working plants, and adjustable desks and chairs for office workers.

OSHA also requires the government to fund research into potentially dangerous working conditions. Current investigations include data collection on a possible relationship between use of computers and miscarriages, back and neck problems, and wrist problems (Carpal Tunnel Syndrome), and the possible health effects of low-energy electromagnetic fields.

Equal Pay Act

The Equal Pay Act was originally passed in 1946 and prohibits wage discrimination based on sex. When a male and a female perform the same job, the Equal Pay Act requires that they be paid the same amount. In 1972, the Act was expanded to cover many more categories of workers, including all government employees.

The Equal Pay Act was passed because women were being paid significantly less than men even when they held the same positions. In 1964, women made 63 cents for every dollar men made. By 1988, women were still only making 68 cents for every dollar men made. Some of the difference is explained by occupational segregation—if service workers are paid less per hour than blue-collar workers, and more service workers are female while more blue-collar workers are male, a wage gap will exist.

However, even when occupation is taken into consideration, women receive significantly less pay than men. For example, using 1988 figures, female lawyers earn 63 percent of what their male counterparts earn, accountant women earn 79 percent of accountant men's salary, female computer programmers earn 81 percent of male programmers' wages, and the difference between female and male managers is 67 percent. As the supply of skilled labor decreases, women have been able to use their bargaining power to reduce the difference. More and more legal cases have resulted in women winning large back-pay awards. AT&T lost one of the first major class-action lawsuits charging pay discrimination. Since then, many other companies have been found guilty in court.

Age Discrimination

Older employees are frequently discriminated against in employment. Companies may resist their higher salary expectations and comparatively limited worklife. The Employment Act of 1967 protects workers 40 and older from discrimination. Given qualifications and experience, workers are to be selected without regard to age. Many applicants 50 and older still find they have difficulty getting hired. So far, the number of age discrimination cases brought to court has been low, although as the population ages, more legal and social pressure to hire employees without regard to age can be expected.

Equal Employment Opportunity

The Civil Rights Act of 1964 (amended in 1972) was written to prohibit discrimination on the basis of race, sex, age, religion, color, or national origin. The section of the Civil Rights Act that refers to employment is called Title VII. It requires equal employment opportunities (EEO) for virtually all public and private employees. Job qualifications must be related to the job, rather than to the sex, age, race, religion, color, or national origin of the job holder. All applicants must be extended an "equal opportunity" to be selected and promoted.

Because employers can no longer legally consider an applicant's sex, race, age or religion, application forms cannot ask for the information. Job seekers are advised not to include pictures or personal information on their resumes.

VOCATIONAL REHABILITATION ACT

The 1973 Vocational Rehabilitation Act added the physically and mentally disabled to the groups protected under Title VII. As long as a worker is able to perform the job tasks "with reasonable accommodation by the employer," mental and physical limitations are not to be considered in selection and promotion decisions.

In 1987, the Supreme Court ruled that those with contagious diseases are covered by the Vocational Rehabilitation Act. The ruling is particularly significant for employees with AIDS. They cannot be dismissed from their job because they have the virus.

VIETNAM-ERA VETERANS

Title VII was amended in 1974 to include veterans of the Vietnam war. Service personnel returning to civilian jobs were experiencing high unemployment rates. The Vietnam-Era Veterans' Readjustment Act included them in the protected groups referred to in the Civil Rights Act.

PREGNANCY DISCRIMINATION

Title VII also prohibits dismissal of women solely because they are pregnant and protects their job security during maternity leaves. Different companies and different states set a variety of maternity leave lengths. The minimum is four weeks. Some companies allow as long as six months. Progressive companies also allow paternity leaves so men can take time to care for their newborns as well. Most parental leave programs are unpaid, although benefits continue.

SEXUAL HARASSMENT

Currently, the largest number of employment lawsuits centers around sexual harassment. An employer can be found guilty of discrimination against women if the organizational climate makes it difficult for women to perform their work. Pictures of nude women, hostile or sexual remarks, and blocking passage through doors are examples of the kind of behavior that leads to charges of sexual harassment.

Congress passed additional amendments to the Civil Rights Act in the 1990–91 legislative session which were vetoed by President Bush. Nondiscrimination and protection of workers' rights continues to be active public policy topics. Human resource managers work to keep their organization's staffing policies and procedures current and reflective of the demands of the society.

Affirmative Action

Through the Executive Order process, U. S. Presidents have the ability to establish policies that carry the weight of law for all government agencies. Since 1965, a series of Executive Orders has established special nondiscrimination requirements which apply to organizations of 15 or more employees that have contracts with the federal government. These organizations are required to "take affirmative action" to counteract the discrimination of the past. In its essence, affirmative action means that, given equal qualifications, the applicant from a minority or protected group must be chosen for the job.

Affirmative action also requires employers to actively recruit minority or protected group applicants. A company might advertise its positions in publications especially read by minority groups or in places where a greater percentage of minority applicants would see them. It might also offer additional training opportunities.

Failure to establish and follow an affirmative action plan will result in the organization losing its federal funds (for example in public education) or its federal contract (for example Boeing's contract with the Defense Department). The Department of Labor is responsible for monitoring affirmative action policies.

LABOR RELATIONS

When an organization's employees are represented by one or more union, the interaction of the organization and the union is referred to as *labor relations*. Approximately 16 percent of all workers are union members. Unions can provide significant benefits for both employees and organizations, although most non-unionized organizations resist the introduction of unions.

In a unionized situation, the policies and procedures that relate to the selection, hiring, reviewing, compensation, and firing of employees are determined through negotiation or bargaining between worker representatives and management representatives. The outcome of bargaining is a contract in which both labor and management are legally bound to perform in certain ways.

As a result, much of the human resource management function is handled by the union in a unionized organization. Both sides to the contractual agreement have greater predictability. Opponents to unionization claim unions result in higher labor costs and significantly reduced managerial flexibility.

Nothing is more important to an organization or to its employees than its management of the human resource. From the organization's point of view, if organizational objectives are to be accomplished, the organization must attract, select, train, and retain qualified people. Changing market conditions and changing population demographics make staffing particularly challenging.

Although large organizations have human resource specialists, all managers are responsible for participating in the the staffing function. Staffing is highly technical, requiring specific knowledge of the legal requirements that affect all employee interactions.

From the employee's point of view, staffing policies have a significant impact on both motivation and ability. Job design, worker selection, and the training the organization offers have a direct impact on worker ability. As the next chapter discusses in detail, appraisal and compensation policies can affect motivation.

Selected Readings

Abrams, A. L., and G. L. Tidwell. 1989. "Affirmative Action." *Business & Economic Review* (Oct/Dec): 27–29.

Coil, Ann. 1984. "Job Matching Brings Out the Best in Employees." *Personnel Journal* (Jan): 61–64.

Fombrun, Charles J., and Robert L. Laud. 1983. "Strategic Issues in Performance Appraisal: Theory and Practice." *Personnel* 60 (6): 23–31.

Ingleshoff, Martha E. 1990. "Managing the New Work Force." *Inc.* (Jan): 78–83.

Keys, Bernard, and Joseph Wolfe. 1988. "Management Education and Development: Current Issues and Emerging Trends." *Journal of Management* 2: 205–229.

Leap, Terry L., William H. Holley, Jr., and Hubert S. Field. 1980. "Equal Employment Opportunity and Its Implications for Personnel Practices in the 1980s." *Labor Law Journal* 31 (11): 669–682.

Longnecker, C. O., J. P. Sims, Jr., and D. A. Gioia. 1987. "Behind the Mask: The Politics of Employee Appraisal." *The Academy of Management Executive* (Aug): 183–193.

Mellon, Craig. 1988. "The Dope on Drug Testing." *Human Resource Executive*, 2 (4): 34–37.

Niehoff, Marilee S. 1983. "Assessment Centers: Decision-Making Information from Non-Test-Based Methods." *Small Group Behavior* 14 (3): 353–358.

Peter, Laurence J., and Raymond Hull. 1969. *The Peter Principle* New York: William Morrow.

Pursell, E. D., M. A. Campion, and S. R. Gaylord. 1980. "Structured Interviewing: Avoiding Selection Problems." *Personnel Journal* (Nov): 904–912.

Schuler, Randall S., Steven P. Galiente, and Susan E. Jackson. 1987. "Matching Effective Human Resource Practices with Competitive Strategy." *Personnel* (Sept): 18–27.

14

Motivation

To achieve their mission, organizations are dependent upon employee productivity or performance. Individual performance is the result of two interacting factors—ability and motivation. Employees enter the organization with some level of ability. The organization can increase that level through training and the efficient organization of tasks and supplies.

Employees also enter the organization with some level of motivation or willingness and desire to perform. As this chapter will discuss, organizations can also influence employee motivation.

Motivation is an internal construct. Somewhat like a reflexive verb, one can only motivate oneself. However, managers can set the stage. Ralph Waldo Emerson said, "Nothing great was ever achieved without enthusiasm." Managers have the challenging task of encouraging enthusiasm in their employees.

MOTIVATION THEORIES

Motivation is the willingness to put forth effort in order to accomplish something. When organizations discuss "motivated employees," of course they mean willingness to put forth effort toward accomplishing *organizational objectives*.

Four major types of theories have been developed for explaining why humans are motivated. *Needs theories* propose that humans put forth effort in order to fulfill needs. *Equity theory* argues that humans are motivated by comparing the results of their efforts with the results others obtain. *Reinforcement theory* sees effort as a natural consequence of learning which behaviors are rewarded and which are not. *Expectancy theory* attempts to integrate elements of the other theories. An understanding of each of these motivation theories will help managers establish the conditions which encourage employee motivation.

Needs Theories

In general, needs theories (sometimes called content theories) attempt to answer the question, "What compels people to action?" Underlying all needs theories is the assumption that humans have inner needs and they act in order to meet them. They are willing to put forth effort so that the organization can meet its goals only because the organization provides opportunities for them to meet their individual needs. Different theorists have combined needs into a variety of different categories. Each provides insight into why humans behave as they do.

MASLOW'S HIERARCHY OF NEEDS

In the early 1950s, Abraham Maslow was practicing psychology and studying what motivates people. He proposed that *only unmet needs motivate*. For example, an employee is motivated by money only when he or she does not have enough. However, once an individual believes enough money is earned to meet financial needs, the promise of a raise will not result in greater effort.

Maslow also argued that needs are hierarchical—that is, some needs are more basic than others. When basic needs are unmet, all of a person's attention is focused on meeting them. Once basic needs are at least partially met, an individual will exert effort to fulfill the next level of needs.

Maslow identified the hierarchy as follows.

1. *Physiological needs.* These most basic needs include water, food, rest, sex, and shelter. Typically, organizations help members meet these needs by paying them wages. They also schedule rest periods and eating periods.

2. *Safety and security needs.* The needs on this next level of the hierarchy include safety from physical and psychological harm. Life insurance, health insurance, job security, and a safe work environment are examples of ways safety needs might be met at work.

3. *Belongingness and love.* This level includes the need to belong. In addition to the need for the affection of others, this level includes the need to love others. In organizations, teamwork and socializing offer ways members might meet these needs.

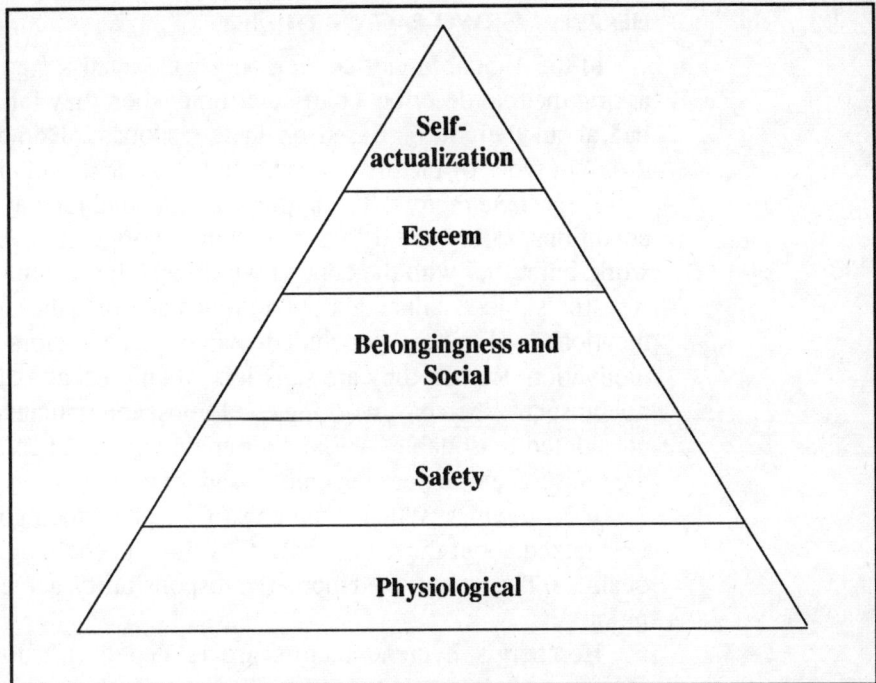

Fig. 14.1 Maslow's Hierarchy of Needs

4. *Esteem.* This level includes needs for self-respect, self-esteem, achievement, and the respect of others. Dale Carnegie's famous book, *How to Win Friends and Influence People*, asserts that the respect of others is a worker's most powerful need. He suggests that managers regularly take the time to let subordinates know how important their contributions are to the organization.

5. *Self-actualization.* This group of needs focuses on personal growth. The need to grow, to feel fulfilled, and to reach one's potential are examples. Self-actualization has been defined as "becoming all that you can be." Training and development programs, new responsibilities, and high quality work may all provide opportunities for organizational members to meet self-actualization needs.

Several management theorists have observed that Maslow's hierarchy is culturally bound. For example, Edwin Nevis (1983) found that belonging is the most important and basic need in China. Physiological and safety needs follow that.

HERZBERG'S TWO-FACTOR THEORY

In the 1950s, Frederick Herzberg conducted a study of professionals, asking them to describe a particular time when they felt especially good or bad about their jobs. Based on their responses, Herzberg identified two different types of factors which he called *hygiene* and *motivator*.

1. *Hygiene factors*. The hygiene factors include pay, benefits, working conditions, safety conditions and other factors that have to do not with the work, but rather with the context within which the work is done. When the research subjects talked about bad times at work, these are the topics they mentioned. Herzberg concluded that hygiene factors do not encourage motivation. Rather, they are satisfiers when present and dissatisfiers when not present. When pay, working conditions, and policies and procedures are considered reasonable, workers are maintained. When the hygiene factors are missing, employees become dissatisfied.

2. *Motivators*. When research subjects described good work incidents, they talked about the actual work they do—its challenging and meaningful qualities. They mentioned increased responsibility, achievement, and recognition.

Herzberg's hygiene factors are related to Maslow's physiological, safety, and belongingness needs. They tend to be tangible and measurable. The motivators are similar to the esteem and self–actualizing level of Maslow's hierarchy. In general, motivators are not quantifiable. Therefore they are harder to "dispense in an organization. The important finding of Herzberg's work is that organizations, in order to have more motivated employees, must provide both hygiene and motivating factors.

ALDERFER'S ERG THEORY

Clayton Alderfer, researching organizational psychology in the late 1960s, agreed with Maslow that needs are hierarchical, although he used three categories of needs rather than five.

Existence needs are similar to Maslow's physiological and safety needs. *Relatedness* needs include Maslow's social need for relationships with others. *Growth* needs for personal creativity and influence are similar to Maslow's esteem and self-actualization need levels. The initials for existence, relatedness, and growth have become the name of the theory—ERG. (See Fig. 14.2 on the following page.)

The significant difference between Maslow's work and Alderfer's is that, whereas Maslow believed only unsatisfied needs motivate, Alderfer held that when higher-level needs cannot be fulfilled, lower-level needs, although satisfied, return. For example, a worker who feels his growth needs are thwarted because of a dead-end job may demand more pay.

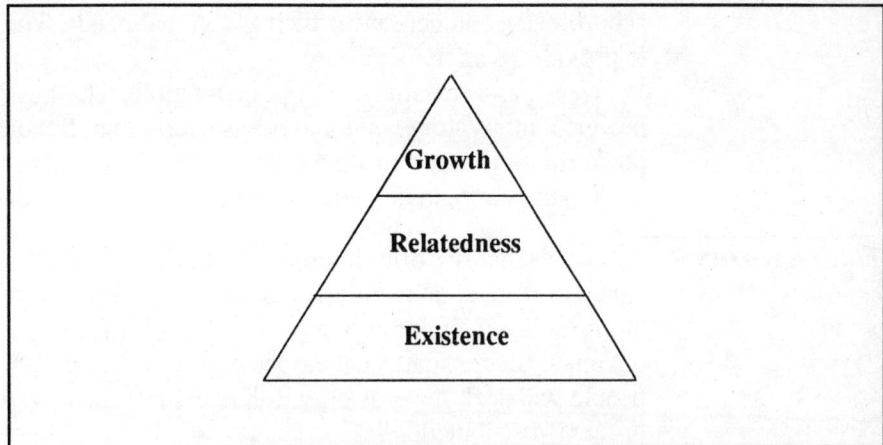

Fig. 14.2 Alderfer's Needs Hierarchy

MCCLELLAND'S NEEDS THEORY

David McClelland has been researching motivation, especially of managers, for twenty years. His observations have led him to conclude that some needs are learned or acquired through interaction with the environment. He has developed a model of three basic human needs—the need for achievement, the need for affiliation, and the need for power.

1. *Need for achievement.* People with a high need for achievement tend to seek frequent and concrete performance feedback, they like challenges, and they want to take personal responsibility for getting things done. Approximately 10 percent of U.S. adults have a high need for achievement. They tend to prefer self-management situations. McClelland found that those with high need for achievement are typically excellent organizational performers.

2. *Need for affiliation.* People with a high need for affiliation value relationships with others. They like socializing, parties, joining organizations, and belonging. They want to be liked by others. People with a high need for affiliation work well on teams and like work which helps others.

3. *Need for power.* People with high power needs like to influence or control others. They tend to be competitive and seek dominance. When individuals use their need for power to work with others, they are likely to be effective managers.

OVERVIEW OF NEEDS THEORIES

These and other needs theories make several very important points. One is that different people have different needs at different times during their lifetime. As a result, an organizational reward may motivate some and not others. The increasing cultural and demographic diversity in the workforce makes the differences even larger. Managers need to pay attention to their subordinates and determine their individual needs. The organization needs to provide a variety of rewards.

Needs and rewards need not be tangible. The boss's respect may be a powerful motivator even though it is nearly undefinable. Some of the most powerful motivators cost the organization nothing financially.

In summary, unmet needs motivate. Fulfilled needs do not motivate.

Equity Theory

Needs theories offer internal, personal reasons why an individual would expend effort to achieve a reward. Equity theory argues that humans are motivated by comparing the results of their efforts with the results others obtain. J. Stacy Adams developed equity theory in 1963. He contends that people will seek rewards only if they believe the rewards will be equitably or fairly distributed.

An important observation which applies to equity theory, or social comparison, is that behavior is the result of *perception*, not *reality*. If a worker believes he works harder than his office mate who receives the same pay, he will act on that perception, whether or not it is objectively true. If the employees of United Parcel Service believe they are paid more than the employees of other shipping service companies, that belief is a more important contribution to motivation than the facts.

Equity theory proposes that individuals are motivated to reduce any perceived inequity. When people perceive an inequity, they will adjust their behavior to reduce the perceived inequity. They might work more slowly or, alternatively, spend more hours at work. Perhaps a worker, perceiving that others get more, would change the outputs rather than the inputs, for example, by requesting a pay increase or taking home office supplies. Still others might adjust their perceptions and reevaluate the comparison, perhaps by choosing different comparison individuals.

Typically, workers perform two comparisons. They compare themselves to others in their organization, considering organization level and task responsibilities. Then they compare themselves with others who do the same kind of work, but in other companies. A software designer at IBM will consider the internal organizational hierarchy and the possible rewards. Do software designers earn more than janitors and less than product managers? Do software designers at IBM all earn similar pay, given education and experience? Do managers work longer hours?

Then the software designer might attend a national convention of computer engineers and talk with others in the same profession. Do IBM software designers earn about the same as MicroSoft software designers? Do they work about the same number of hours per week? Do they get about the same equipment and staff support?

Reinforcement Theory

Reinforcement theory is based primarily on the research of psychologist B.F. Skinner. He contends that behavior is the result of past behavior and its consequences. When a behavior is rewarded with a desired outcome, it is likely to be repeated. When a behavior results in no reward, it tends to disappear or be "extinguished." Skinner suggests avoiding punishment because it is likely to result in rebellious reaction.

When Skinner's reinforcement theory is applied in organizations, it is called organizational behavior modification. Behavior modification is based on two fundamental concepts. The first is that people act in ways they find personally most rewarding. The second is that behavior can be shaped and determined by controlling the rewards. Skinner indicates that the rewards should follow the behavior as immediately as possible so that the link between behavior and reward is clear.

The quarterly *Journal of Organizational Behavior Management* reports almost exclusively results of the application of reinforcement theory to organizations. Although reinforcement theory has proven itself as an effective motivation tool, it has its opponents. Critics argue that it is manipulative and autocratic. Skinner, in 1972, responded, "We are all controlled by the world in which we live, and part of that world has been and will be constructed by men. The question is this: are we to be controlled by accidents, by tyrants, or by ourselves in effective cultural design?"

Expectancy Theory

Victor Vroom, a management scholar, developed expectancy theory, which offers an integrated model of motivation. His model,

$$\text{Motivation} = \text{Expectancy} \times \text{Valence} \times \text{Instrumentality},$$

explains motivation as being the result of an individual's goals and the expectations of achieving them.

Expectancy is a person's perception of the probability that effort will lead to performance. If an employee believes that working harder will result in greater output, he or she has a high expectancy. Sometimes students performing in groups believe that harder work will make no difference if others in the group do not work harder. Those students have low expectancy. Some assembly-line work leaves workers with an expectancy of zero. Because their contribution is so specialized, it is difficult to see any relationship between effort and end product. The lower the expectancy, the lower the motivation.

Instrumentality is the perceived link between productivity and reward. End-of-quarter bonuses are offered by companies to increase instrumentality. High production and sales will lead to higher pay. Alternatively, a new worker at a factory where seniority rather than performance determines pay, vacation times, and job assignments may see very little connection between performance and desired reward. That worker would have low instrumentality.

Valence refers to the value the person places on the perceived outcome of effort. The organization may offer a promotion to the worker who performs best on a task. If one worker has high esteem needs, the valence of the promotion outcome or reward would be high. If, on the other hand, a worker has high belongingness needs and worries that a promotion would result in lost friendships, valence for that worker would be low.

As long as expectancy, instrumentality, and valence are greater than 0, some motivation should be present. Expectancy theory has been widely applied in organizations because it encourages managers to do what they can to increase the links between performance, outcome, and reward.

MOTIVATION AND REWARDS

Increasing instrumentality requires that the organizational members see a direct link between performance and reward. Steven Kerr, an academic, wrote a widely read article entitled, "On the Folly of Rewarding A while Expecting B." In his article, he discusses how medical doctors are rewarded whenever patients are sick and need treatment. Of course the patient hopes the doctor will make him or her well, but the doctor is only paid when the patient is not feeling well. Making sure that what is rewarded is what is desired is an essential part of effective motivation.

Intrinsic/ Extrinsic Rewards

There are two categories or kinds of rewards. An *extrinsic reward* is given to someone by others. Typically, it is something outside the task being performed. For example, pay, benefits, promotions, and size of office are all extrinsic rewards. When a child gets a popsicle for cleaning the bedroom, that is an extrinsic reward.

Intrinsic rewards are more closely associated with the work being done. They arise from within the worker. For example, personal pride in a job well done is an intrinsic reward. If the child with the clean room now has a feeling of accomplishment, that is an intrinsic reward.

Research indicates that intrinsic rewards are more powerful motivators than extrinsic rewards—as Herzberg predicted in the two-factor theory. Children who get stickers for doing well on spelling exams are not as motivated to learn spelling as children who are rewarded for good spelling by being able to use their new words to write something.

Performance/ Satisfaction

Interestingly, researchers have found that satisfaction does not lead to greater performance. Happy workers do not produce more because they are happy. Actually the relationship works backwards to the widely-held assumption that satisfaction leads to performance. Good quality performance leads to an intrinsic reward-satisfaction.

The chances are excellent that dissatisfied, unhappy workers are thwarted in their attempts to perform by poor organization. Perhaps tools break down or supplies do not arrive on time or cumbersome policies and procedures slow their work.

Timing of Rewards

A great deal of the literature on motivation and rewards stresses the importance of providing a reward shortly after the performance so the performer sees the link between performance and reward clearly. Behavior modification research has specifically tested the results of immediate reward versus delayed reward and consistent reward versus intermittent reward. A problem exists, however, in providing rapid feedback and rewards—people begin focusing on the short run at the expense of the long run. The average tenure of a *Fortune 500* chief executive officer is three years. Each quarter's earnings have a profound effect on the stock price. When the system rewards short–term performance, it is folly to expect long-term vision.

Because motivation or the willingness to expend effort is internal to individuals, management's task of increasing the conditions under which they will be motivated is a difficult one. The first step is recognizing that people act in order to satisfy their personal needs. The second step is recognizing that different people have different needs.

Managers must then make it possible for employees to meet their personal needs by performing organizationally-desired tasks. Clarifying the links between goals, performance, and rewards is a large part of effective motivation. Goal setting works. So does behavior modification.

The key to effective motivating may be planning. A manager needs to know the subordinates, know what needs to be done in the organization, and plan how to provide meaningful rewards in a timely and equitable manner.

Selected Readings

Adams, J. Stacy. 1963. "Toward an Understanding of Inequity." *Journal of Abnormal and Social Psychology* 67 (5): 422–436.

Alderfer, C. P. 1972. *Existence, Relatedness, and Growth: Human Needs in Organizational Settings.* New York: Free Press.

Herzberg, Frederick. 1966. *Work and the Nature of Man.* New York: World Publishing.

Luthans, Fred, and Robert Kreitner. 1985. *Organizational Behavior Modification and Beyond.* Glenview, IL: Scott, Foresman.

Maslow, Abraham H. 1970. *Motivation and Personality*, 2nd ed. New York: Harper & Row.

McClelland, David C. 1961. *The Achieving Society.* New York: Van Nostrand.

Porter, Lyman W., and Edward E. Lawler III. 1968. *Managerial Attitudes and Performance*. Homewood, IL: Richard D. Irwin.

Robbins, Anthony. 1986. *Unlimited Power*. New York: Fawcett Columbine.

Skinner, B. F. 1971. *Beyond Freedom and Dignity*. New York: Alfred A. Knopf.

Tarkenton, Fran, with Tad Tuleja. 1986. *How to Motivate People*. New York: Harper & Row.

Vroom, Victor. 1964. *Work and Motivation*. New York: Wiley.

15

Group Dynamics

As the previous chapters have discussed, organizations provide a planned mechanism for achieving objectives. Organizations also act as social entities. Within most organizations, a maze of informal relationships and interactions is superimposed on the formal relationships.

These informal organizations or groups often have tremendous impact on employee attitudes and performance. As a result, managers need an understanding of groups—both the formal aspects and the informal ones.

Much of the work of organizations is accomplished by groups. Groups have special dynamics which are different from the dynamics of one-on-one relationships. Managers must manage groups as expertly as they manage individuals.

FORMAL AND INFORMAL GROUPS

In the assembly-line organization of the Industrial Age, workers completed specialized tasks independently. Most management involved supervising individual workers at work. Information Age organizations are, as discussed in chapter 10, increasingly meeting objectives through project and task teams. Managing in the new team environment, as author/scholar Hischhorn suggests in his 1991 book of that name, requires managers to have a good understanding of how teams function. Some groups are more effective than others. Some support the objectives of the organization, but some do not.

Formal Groups

Two principal types of groups exist. The *formal* group is intentionally created by managers and has specific assigned responsibilities for meeting organizational objectives. Project teams and safety committees are examples. Formal groups are part of the organization's structure. More and more businesses are moving to a "flexible teams" structure.

Formal work groups can be permanent, as in the case of divisions or departments, or they can be temporary. A committee might be charged with rewriting company policy on accepting personal checks. Once the new policies have been approved, the committee dissolves.

Informal Groups

In every organization larger than two members, informal organizations are certain to arise (for reasons which will be addressed later in the chapter). *Informal* groups do not have a formal performance purpose and are not part of the organizational structure. Examples would include a group of people who play bridge at lunch, a group who plans to get a union going, and a group who shares work ideas.

Informal groups meet many personal and organizational needs. They provide a mechanism for meeting social needs—getting together with people of similar likes. They may speed communication. In crisis situations, they help solve problems.

Whereas formal groups focus on tasks, informal groups focus on relationships. When the informal groups support the formal groups, the organization will be especially effective. When they do not match well, counterproductive consequences are likely to occur. For example, suppose a company has a formal project team whose goal is to redesign the company's top-selling product so that it can be assembled faster using more automation. If two of the project team's members are on a bowling team with two workers from the assembly department, they may have an informal goal to save their bowling teammates' jobs.

GROUP FORMATION

Groups, both formal and informal, are most likely to occur when individuals share the following.

1. *Common goals.* Groups result in synergy—the members' combined efforts are larger than if each member worked independently. Three people pushing together can move a car further and more easily than if each person pushed alone, one after the other. When goal achievement is important,

people are likely to join with others who share the same goals and use synergy to help reach them.

2. *Common needs*. Time-share is a growing industry which gets people who share a common need for vacation homes together in groups. Four families might jointly own a lodge at Lake Tahoe or a beach house on the French Riviera. Then they share the time, each family having use of the facilities one fourth of the time. Groups help members fill common needs.

3. *Common interests*. People interested in learning about nature are likely to join the Sierra Club. Bridge players are likely to get together during lunch. Golfers might have a standing Saturday morning tee-time. Shared interests bring people together in groups.

4. *Physical proximity*. People who are around each other learn to like each other and want to spend more time together. Most people know the neighbor who lives across the street from them and the one who lives on the side their driveway is on. Rather than "familiarity breeds contempt," research demonstrates that proximity contributes to group formation.

5. *Collective power*. People believe the adage "there is strength in numbers." When individuals want to multiply their power, they are likely to form groups. For example, workers join unions so their collective power will give them leverage in negotiations with management. Collective power also helps individuals meet security needs. Neighborhood Watch programs work because together neighbors can keep watch over the neighborhood even while some of the neighbors are absent.

6. *Status*. As many marketers have discovered, status and prestige are great selling points. American Express advertises its charge card with the phrase, "Membership has its privileges." When a group is perceived as having high status, individuals want to join. As Woody Allen puts it, "I'd never join a group who would have me as a member."

7. *Self-esteem*. Especially within certain fields or industries, membership in a professional group can help a person meet esteem needs. For example, accountants typically strive to become Certified Public Accountants or Certified Managerial Accountants. Production and operations management people frequently join the American Production and

Inventory Control Society. Belonging to certain groups makes people feel good about themselves.

8. *Affiliation*. Groups help members meet their needs to belong. Those people who say they would continue working if they won the lottery probably value the relationships they have with the people where they work. Students who join fraternities or sororities do so largely for affiliation.

Groups, like interpersonal relationships, go through predictable stages in their development. The group must develop a "personality" and set of behaviors expected of its members before it can truly function effectively. Groups usually go through five stages in reaching maturity although they do not necessarily move through them smoothly and in order. In fact, many groups disband before they become fully mature.

Joining or Forming

In the first stage, members of the group decide how committed they want to be. Members are focused on the group's task and on defining or learning acceptable group behaviors. Members' energy is exhausted clarifying the task and getting to know one another—learning the ropes.

Subgrouping

As part of clarifying who the group is and what it hopes to achieve, subgroups of people who share common views are likely to arise. With a group as small as three members, subgroups will form. The subgroups help the group decide more clearly what the task is and what the group norms for behavior are. Cohesiveness increases and so does productivity.

Sometimes group cohesiveness appears to go up because members implicitly agree to keep conflict and disagreement to a minimum. Important issues may go unresolved.

Confrontation

As members of a group become more comfortable with their group identity, they are willing to express disagreement, especially if they know a subgroup agrees with them. Members are most likely to disagree about the group's purpose, the best methods for achieving the purpose, and how much time members are expect to devote to the group.

If the conflict goes unresolved, or becomes focused on certain people, the group is likely to dissolve. On the other hand, if the conflict is handled constructively, the group moves rapidly toward greater maturity and effectiveness. The expression of diverse viewpoints leads the group to more creative solutions.

Individual Differentiation

An important step in reaching group maturity is allowing group members to retain (or perhaps regain) their individuality. In addition to their roles as group members, they are given the autonomy to pursue personal needs and objectives. Groups at this stage are very effective at getting tasks accomplished. The group is secure in its identity. Very few groups reach this stage.

Collaboration

When group members are free to be themselves and trust that the group will last, the group becomes fully mature and especially effective. Members know they can count on each other to achieve the group's goals. They collaborate. When the group is successful, the members of a mature group believe that they are, thereby, also individually successful. Because they seek *shared* power, members of a mature group work effectively together for everyone's good.

Even fewer groups reach this stage of maturation. Because this stage is so much more effective, managers may want to assist groups, especially long-term formal groups, to achieve it. They can do so by encouraging constructive handling of conflict, by clarifying member similarities as well as member differences, and by manipulating the physical environment such that group members are in closer physical proximity.

Adjourning

Groups formed to accomplish specific tasks go through a special stage when their tasks are complete and the group prepares to adjourn. Rather than task performance, they focus on wrapping-up activities. Some group members will focus on accomplishment; others will focus on loss of friendship and interaction. Agreeing on a specific future time to meet and talk about the project will help all group members let go and become productive members of new groups.

FACTORS AFFECTING GROUP PERFORMANCE

In addition to the stage of maturity, other factors influence how effective a group is. Understanding these factors can help managers manage group performance.

Group Size

The number of members in a group influences how the group functions and the kinds of dysfunctional conflict that can arise. For example, disagreements in groups of two (called dyads) will most likely lead to one winner and one loser. Dyads are frequently characterized by tension and anxiety.

In groups of three (called triads), there is a recurring tendency to form coalitions—two against one. The "one" is likely to feel resentful. Usually in triads, the coalitions form and reform constantly, making the group inherently unstable.

With four-person groups, voting is not an effective way of settling disputes because tie votes are inevitable. In fact, research demonstrates that conflict is always greater in groups with an even number of members.

When groups become larger than seven, they are considered "large groups." The dynamics of large groups are quite different from the dynamics of small groups. Research findings about large groups indicate that coordination is difficult, that some members will become passive, and that the more dominant group members are likely to become aggressive. The benefit of large groups is that more information and points of view may be considered in problem solving.

The conclusions of research on group process indicate that:

1. Groups with five members are the most effective in the largest number of situations.

2. In a conflict situation, when consensus is desired, three to five group members and no formal leader will be most effective for solving the conflict.

3. When a particularly complex problem must be solved, seven to twelve group members, each of whom has different information and biases, will result in the best quality decision. This finding is especially true when the group has a formal leader.

Group Member Roles

In the 1950s, researcher Robert Bales addressed the importance of various roles in group dynamics. A *role* is a total pattern of expected behavior. In life, each individual plays many roles: spouse, friend, executive, good listener, parent, child. Roles include language patterns and dress styles, as well as behaviors. For example, in the Silicon Valley of California where many high tech computer companies have their headquarters, CEOs are expected to drive a Mercedes, even if they would prefer a Ford. They are also expected to wear traditional business suits while their subordinates are expected to wear jeans and tee-shirts. The group of people who share the pattern of expected behavior is referred to as the *role set*.

Bales concluded that all groups need members who will take task-focused roles—seeing that the objectives are met—and members who will assume relationship-focused roles—seeing that tensions are released and that group members get along.

Bales observed another important characteristic of group dynamics. Groups have leaders. Even when a group has a formal leader, for example the committee chairperson or the department manager, it will also have an informal leader. The group will choose as its informal leader the person who a) talks the most frequently, and b) talks for the longest duration—no matter what the quality of the input is. If the formal leader and the informal leader have a shared sense of the group's goals, the group will be more effective than if they disagree about the group's direction. When the formal and informal leader disagree strongly, the group is more likely to follow the informal leader.

Group Norms

All groups have *norms*, which are acceptable standards of behavior shared by the group's members. Different groups might have quite different norms. For example, in the classroom group, students are expected to arrive promptly for class. When a particular student arrives late three days in a row, the other students will apply first nonverbal and then verbal pressure to get the tardy student to follow the group norm. On the other hand, when students are invited to a student party, the norm is to arrive about one hour after the stated party time. If a student were to arrive "on time," the host would probably not be ready for guests.

DEVELOPMENT OF NORMS

Norms are unwritten codes of behavior which arise informally through interaction of group members. They usually develop in one of the following four ways.

1. They are explicitly stated by supervisors or co-workers. Reward systems must support explicitly stated norms.

2. They are communicated through myths about the organization's history. Joseph Campbell and other researchers have concluded that myth and symbols are the fastest way to communicate norms, especially to new members.

3. They are repeated initial patterns of behavior. In *Home Away From Home*, Janet Geringer Waititz discusses how people repeat their childhood or family roles at work. Oldest children become very responsible bosses, youngest children tend to be more creative and playful. Children of alcoholic parents try to take control. Behavioral norms from home are repeated at work.

4. They are carried over from previous situations. If the committee which put on the 30-year reunion had certain norms, the 35-year reunion committee is likely to repeat them, especially if some of the committee members are the same. New employees frequently say, "Well, at my last job this is the way we did it."

New group members gradually become integrated into the group by learning the group norms. The Hawthorne experiments, discussed in chapter 2, concluded that group members, in addition to nonverbal and verbal pressure, would even resort to hitting a worker who did not follow the group norms.

CHARACTERISTICS OF NORMS

In 1976, scholar J. R. Hackman identified five characteristics of norms.

1. Norms represent the structural characteristics of the group. They give a group its personality. The personality of a group is referred to as its culture.

2. Norms apply to behavior, not to private thoughts and feelings. As long as group members comply with the norms, they can think anything they want about them.

3. Norms arise only to control behavior which a majority of the group members believe to be important.

4. Although norms typically arise slowly, they can also develop and be followed rapidly in a crisis situation.

5. Not all norms apply to all group members equally. For example, star atheletes are typically held to all the team norms, whereas support players are not necessarily. Female managers are sometimes held to different behavioral norms than their male counterparts.

GROUP THINK

An interesting research finding is that group norms, especially in groups where the members are highly attracted to one another, are such powerful controllers of behavior that people will often conform to a majority opinion even if it is clearly false. This process is known as *Group Think*. History is replete with examples of groups making faulty decisions because no one was willing to disagree with or question a decision that had become normative. Probably the most frequently analyzed example of Group Think was President John Kennedy's decision to invade the Bay of Pigs. He and his top advisors discussed the plan several times. Even though the idea was a very weak one, once it was proposed, no one was willing to speak out against it and risk the disapproval of the other group members. The Watergate Hotel break-in of the Nixon presidency is another example of Group Think. Scholar Irving Janis has studied the Group Think phenomenon extensively. He concludes that a group where the Group Think process is likely to occur has such cohesiveness that there are no dissenting opinions, perceives itself as invulnerable, rationalizes its actions, and has an unquestioned belief that the group's actions are morally correct. When conformity to group norms leads to acceptance of faulty decisions or unethical behavior, it becomes dangerous.

THE MANAGER AND GROUP NORMS

Many managers focus their attention on controlling the behavior of their subordinates. That kind of managing is never-ending. A much more effective use of managerial time is to influence the organizational norms. When a norm that supports the organizational mission is established, group members will control their own behavior. Understanding norms, how they arise, and how they shape behavior is a more effective use of managerial energy.

Status

Status, or *social ranking of prestige*, plays an important role in the effectiveness of groups. The higher the perceived status of a group, the more others will want to join it. Business students tend to want to attend Stanford, Wharton, or Harvard business schools because those schools have high status. Students who are interested in joining fraternities or sororities know which organizations on their campus have the highest status. Group members will feel considerable tension and anxiety if they are not in a group whose status matches their perceived personal status.

Group Cohesiveness

Group cohesiveness is the degree to which members are attracted to one another and share the group's goals. Groups whose members get along, cooperate, and like each other—who have high cohesiveness—tend to be more productive in reaching the group's objectives. From the organization's perspective, when the group's goals support the organization's goals, a highly cohesive group is especially effective.

EXTERNAL THREAT

Several factors contribute to the cohesiveness of groups. One is external threat. When the members of a group are threatened by outsiders, cohesion goes way up. Employees of companies involved in hostile takeover attempts become very protective of one another and the organization. People trapped in an elevator frequently emerge as a very close-knit group. When a boss pushes too hard on subordinates, they are likely to become cohesive in a collective resistance to him or her.

FREQUENCY OF CONTACT

The more frequently members of a group get together, the more likely they are to have a highly cohesive group. When "best buddies" from high school move to different towns, the affection may remain, but the sense of group diminishes.

HOMOGENEITY

The more alike the members of a group are, the higher their cohesion is likely to be. Work groups of one sex, race, or age are usually more cohesive than mixed groups. In a factory with much cultural diversity, it is likely that the different lunch groups will be divided along racial or ethnic lines. People feel more comfortable when they are around others with whom they identify.

NEED SATISFACTION

To some degree, the only reason people join groups is to satisfy needs. The more effectively a group can help its members satisfy their needs, the more committed to the group the members will be.

GROUP SIZE

As was mentioned earlier, smaller groups tend to be more effective. To a large degree, the higher cohesiveness of smaller groups is what makes them more effective than large groups. As group size gets larger, group homogeneity decreases and so does frequency of interaction. These effects all serve to reduce group cohesion in larger groups.

TYPES OF WORK GROUPS

The synergy of people working together makes groups effective. Research indicates that as problems become more complex, group decision-making quality surpasses the best individual decision-making quality. Managers can take advantage of what they know about group dynamics and incorporate formal groups into the organizational structure. Some types of work groups occur frequently in organizations.

Command Groups

Command groups consist of managers and their subordinates. A purchasing manager and the employees who work in the purchasing department would be an example of a command group. Because the leader of each command group is also a member of a higher-level group, communication and coordination are enhanced. Rensis Likert, a management scholar, referred to the leader/member connections as *linking pins*.

Task Groups

Task groups, sometimes called project teams or committees, are formal groups formed for a specific purpose. When members are chosen for these groups, they are given a charge or task to address. Some groups are relatively permanent. They deal with ongoing issues and are called *standing committees*. In a university, there is usually a library committee which makes recommendations about library purchases. Although members of the committee may change, the committee and its task remains constant.

Some task groups are only temporary. They are created to deal with either a short-term problem or a one-time problem. This type of formal group is called an *ad hoc committee*. If a company is considering whether to build a new factory or stay in the old one and remodel, it might put together an ad hoc committee to study the issue and make a recommendation. Once the committee's report is complete, the group dissolves.

Quality Circles

An approach to group work widely used in Japan and increasingly used in the U.S. is the quality circle. A *quality circle* is a voluntary group of three to twelve employees who perform the same kind of work or work in the same physical area. They meet regularly on company time to identify and solve problems affecting their work or work area. Some of the problems are minor—how can we keep the bathrooms stocked with toilet paper. Some of the problems have major impact on corporate productivity—how can we reduce the time it takes to manufacture this product.

The organization makes a commitment to provide resources for implementing solutions. The members make a commitment of their time, energy, and caring to work on problems not necessarily directly related to their jobs.

Quality circles got their name because the overall objective of these groups is to improve product and service quality. Usually a quality circle has a professional leader whose only job is to help the group with its process. These leaders are usually referred to as *facilitators* since they do not have command authority, but rather do things like get answers to questions and make sure group members are listening carefully to one another. Quality circles are most effective in manufacturing organizations.

Groups form whenever people are in proximity to one another. Strongly cohesive groups can have a large impact on the expected behavior or norms of group members.

When group norms are supportive of organization goals, the energy generated by the dynamics within a group can move the organization rapidly toward its objectives.

When group norms run counter to organizational norms, it is helpful for a manager to understand those factors that encourage or discourage high group cohesion. Managers can influence the formation of groups, but they would be foolish to try to stop their formation. Influencing group norms is a much more effective use of managerial talent.

SELECTED READINGS

Crawford, Richard D. 1991. *In the Era of Human Capital.* New York: Harper-Business.

Feldman, Daniel C., and Hugh J. Arnold. 1983. *Managing Individual and Group Behavior in Organizations.* New York: McGraw-Hill.

Hischhorn, W. 1991. *Managing in the New Team Environment: Skills, Tools, and Methods.* Reading, MA: Addison-Wesley.

Homans, G. 1950. *The Human Group.* New York: Harcourt Brace.

Janis, Irving. 1982. *Victims of Group Think*. 2nd ed. Boston: Houghton Mifflin.

Kets de Vries, Manfred F. R. and Danny Miller. 1990. *The Neurotic Organization*. New York: HarperBusiness.

Lawler, Edward E. III, & Susan A. Mohrman. 1987. "Quality Circles: After the Honeymoon." *Organizational Dynamics* (Spring): 42–54.

Le Play, Frederic. 1982. *On Family, Work, and Social Change*. Chicago: University of Chicago Press.

Likert, Rensis. 1961. *New Patterns of Management*. New York: McGraw-Hill.

Mills, T. M. 1967. *The Sociology of Small Groups*. Englewood Cliffs, NJ: Prentice-Hall.

Ouchi, William G. 1981. *Theory Z*. Reading, MA: Addison-Wesley.

Waititz, Janet Geringer. 1987. *Home Away From Home*. Pompano, FL: Health Communications Publications.

Wood, Robert, Frank Hall, and Koya Azumi. 1983. "Evaluating Quality Circles: The American Application" *California Management Review* (Fall): 42–45.

16

Leadership: Power and Personal Influence

*T*his book, like most management texts, is organized according to management functions—large categories of tasks that must be accomplished in order for an organization to meet its objectives. The implication is that managers are responsible for planning, organizing, staffing, motivating, and controlling, and that specialized knowledge exists for helping them succeed.

This chapter and the next one address how "leaders" are different from or similar to "managers." This chapter takes a look at the more philosophical issues that surround leadership and power. Chapter 17 reports the major research in the field of leadership.

LEADERSHIP DEFINED

Nearly every scholar who has researched leadership has defined it slightly differently. To begin, the distinction between managers and leaders needs to be clarified. *Managers* are appointed. They have legitimate or position power. Their ability to influence others arises from their formal authority. *Leaders* may be appointed, or alternatively, they may emerge from the group. Their ability to influence others arises from other bases of power—their personality or their expert knowledge.

A group may have both a manager and a leader, although the ideal situation would be that all managers were also leaders. Everyone who has ever observed managers has seen that, at the same hierarchical level, some managers are able to accomplish much more than others. While the position power for managers at the same level is the same, some managers are using power and influence more effectively—they are leaders.

Arthur Jago, a scholar interested in leadership theory, defines *leadership* as "both a process and a property. The process of leadership is the use of noncoercive influence to direct and coordinate the activities of the members of an organized group toward the accomplishment of group objectives. As a property, leadership is the set of qualities or characteristics attributed to those who are perceived to successfully employ such influence."

In his book, *Lead, Follow, or Get Out of the Way*, practitioner and consultant Jim Lundy says that the ultimate criterion of a leader is having followers. "A person who has subordinates but no followers is not a leader. Subordinates who are not followers may be viewed as resources to be managed—and that's just the view taken by a supervisor who is not a leader."

These definitions indicate that leaders somehow get more from those they work with than managers or administrators do. Obviously, organizations are interested in improving their productivity, so the topic of leadership is especially interesting to practicing managers. In this chapter, why and how leaders might engender greater productivity will be addressed.

POWER AND INFLUENCE

Throughout the definitions of management and leadership, the terms power and influence are used.

Power

Power is the *ability* to do—to exert influence on others. It is attached to a person, not to a role. (Remember from chapter 11 that *authority* is the legitimate *right* to exert influence on others based on position. It is attached to a role, not to a person. Managers have authority.)

Psychiatrist Rollo May said that the seed of power lies within everyone—some people swell with it; others grow with it. Leaders use power to grow and to help others grow with them.

Influence

Influence is the actual *exertion* of power. Influence causes change in behavior. A person can have power or the ability to exert influence without choosing to use it. Influence implies the person has chosen to use it.

Sources of Power

Chapter 11 discussed authority relationships and introduced sources of power as identified by French and Raven. By way of review, power arises from legitimate position, the ability to reward, and the ability to coerce, all of which can be given to a person by the organization, from the strength of others' regard or liking, and from expertise, all of which must be earned. Author and business consultant Elwood Chapman refers to these power bases as role power, personality power, and knowledge power.

Freedom and Control

Power is a function of social relationships. In a relationship, one person's power is the result of another person's dependencies. A manager can only exercise meaningful reward power, for example, if the other person wants something. The reason the effective use of power is so difficult is that people do not like to be dependent, to give up their freedom. They fear the power of others and sometimes they fear having power themselves. Leaders must return something to followers in exchange for their dependency and loss of control.

PERSONAL POWER

As was mentioned in chapter 14 on motivation, some people have a greater need for power than others. In order to be an effective leader, a person must be willing to garner and use power.

Additional Sources of Power

A leader can use several strategies for securing additional power through politics. *Politics* is a network of interactions by which power is transferred or "brokered." Although many people think of politics as somehow indirect and under-the-table, the idea of exchanging power and favors is not inherently bad. In fact, a great deal is accomplished in organizations because power and favors are traded.

NETWORKING

Networking refers to building interpersonal relationships, usually in order to share information informally. Getting to know influential people typically increases an individual's personal power, and gives him or her access to information and influence not otherwise available. Rotary International, a service organization, lost its legal right to exclude female members. The females who brought the case to court argued successfully that men built such strong networks as members of Rotary that they had an unfair power advantage over females in terms of employment opportunities.

COALESCING

As discussed in chapter 14, one of the reasons individuals join groups is because there is strength, or power, in numbers. Coalescing, or coming together in alliances, increases power and influence. Although their philosophies and methods are very different, Earth First! and Sierra Club are both organizations concerned with saving the environment. Usually the organizations are critical of each other. However, when a particularly important piece of legislation is before Congress, they might form a coalition to create greater lobbying power.

CO-OPTING

The especially astute organizational politicker will try to co-opt a powerful opponent. *Co-opt* means to create an alliance with powerful others such that they become part of the group. For example, an influential manager known to have reservations about the company's decision to build a new factory may be included on a committee that will work with the architect on designing the interior. The chances are that participation in the project will reduce the manager's resistance and increase the influence of the group.

ACCEPTING THE RIGHT PROJECT

Some projects are nothing but trouble for the person who takes them on. The bearer of bad tidings will find it difficult not to be associated with the bad news. On the other hand, some projects result in media attention, name recognition, and opportunities for more networking. Such projects build a person's power base.

Creating a Vacuum

The biggest difference between a manager and a leader may be how they use the power they have. "Managing subordinates" implies that the manager is set off from the subordinates and is *pushing* them to perform. Leaders appear to understand the law of physics that says nature abhors a vacuum. Leaders get out in front and *pull*. They communicate a vision, listen carefully to subordinates, jointly set goals with them, and offer meaningful rewards for reaching them. Their pulling creates a vacuum, and their subordinates become followers, rushing in to fill the space behind the leader.

The Need for Power

When David McClelland was studying those with a high need for power (see chapter 14), he identified two very different types of people with high power needs. The first type strives for dominance—for power *over* others. They are more likely to use coercive power and to be autocratic and directive. They have very low needs for affiliation and avoid joining groups. They are likely to exploit others.

The second type of high-power-need person is participative and strives for power *with* others. They are good at engendering loyalty and openness in their subordinates. It is this type of need for power which results in good leadership skills. As the next section will detail, these people hold more positive assumptions about subordinates.

Philosophies of Human Nature

Douglas McGregor, organizational consultant in the 1950s and 1960s, proposed that the way managers deal with subordinates is based on a set of assumptions they hold about people in general and employees in particular. He identified a basically negative view which he labeled Theory X and a basically positive view labeled Theory Y.

THEORY X

Under Theory X, managers believe the following assumptions are true about people.

1. Employees inherently dislike work and will, whenever possible, avoid it.
2. As a result, employees must be coerced or threatened into achieving desired goals.
3. Employees avoid responsibility, preferring to be directed by others.
4. Most workers' greatest need is for security. They display little ambition and take few risks.

THEORY Y

Another set of managers believe the following alternative assumptions are true about people.

1. Employees find work as natural as rest or play.
2. As a result, employees will exercise self-direction and self-control if they know what the objectives are.
3. Employees will accept and even seek greater responsibility.
4. Creativity and the ability to make good decisions are widely dispersed throughout the population.

Self-Fulfilling Prophecy

The self-fulfilling prophecy has a very powerful influence on people's behavior. Essentially, the self-fulfilling prophecy says one will experience in life what one expects to experience. There are three reasons why the self-fulfilling prophecy works.

PERCEPTION

First, humans decide what is real in the world by using their senses (sight, hearing, taste, feel, smell, and balance), and human senses are somewhat limited. For example, humans see less than 10 percent of all light wave lengths. Dogs have the ability to perceive smell 40,000 times better than humans. Human senses consider only limited information and so make mistakes. What people perceive is real and true may or may not be.

BEHAVIOR

Second, people react to or behave as a result of what they *perceive* to be true, whether or not it is really true. As an extreme example, people suffering from anorexia believe themselves to be grossly fat even while they are dying of starvation. They respond to their *perception* by dieting more.

ASSUMPTIONS

Third, what people expect to perceive, they are more likely to perceive. Their expectations are based on their assumptions about what it true. Thus, managers who believe Theory X to be true will see evidence that they are correct, and they will act on that "evidence." Managers who believe the assumptions of Theory Y will find their own supportive evidence.

The question is, which set of assumptions most reflects reality? To some degree, different situations lead to different conclusions. A growing number of psychologists, management practitioners, and academic scholars are coming to the conclusion that although managers may believe in Theory X assumptions and in the necessity of having power over others, leaders always make Theory Y assumptions.

QUALITIES OF LEADERS

As the next chapter will discuss, researchers have been unable to develop a list of personal traits which, when present, would predict leadership ability. However, there do appear to be some behavioral consistencies among leaders. In his book, *Leadership*, Elwood Chapman provides the following comparison.

Managers	Leaders
Protect their operations	Advance their operations
Accept responsibility	Seek responsibility
Minimize risks	Take calculated risks
Accept speaking opportunities	Generate speaking opportunities
Set reasonable goals	Set "unreasonable" goals

Pacify problem employees	Challenge problem employees
Strive for a comfortable working environment	Strive for an exciting working environment
Use power cautiously	Use power forcefully
Delegate cautiously	Delegate enthusiastically
View workers as employees	View workers as potential followers

Based on four years of research, Gary Yukl identified the following traits and skills as characteristic of most successful leaders. (From his book, *Leadership in Organizations*, p. 70)

Traits	**Skills**
Adaptable to situations	Clever (intelligent)
Alert to social environment	Conceptually skilled
Ambitious and achievement oriented	Creative
Assertive	Diplomatic and tactful
Cooperative	Fluent speaker
Decisive	Knowledgeable about group task
Dependable	Organized
Dominant (desire to influence others)	Persuasive
Energetic (high energy level)	Socially skilled
Persistent	
Self-confident	
Tolerant of stress	
Willing to assume responsibility	

A Performance Systems survey of over 2000 managers asked what characteristics contribute to their respect for leaders. The top five answers, as reported in Jim Lundy's *Lead, Follow, or Get Out of the Way* include these (p. 14).

1. Communicates, allows input, is willing to listen.

2. Is interested, appreciative, complimentary, supportive, humanistic, considerate.

3. Displays honesty, integrity, trustworthiness.

4. Is objective, open-minded, tolerant, rational, reasonable, fair.

5. Delegates, trusts subordinates, allows room to achieve.

A 1988 *Fortune* magazine article reported that consultants, academics, and executives agree that the following seven guidelines, in aggregate, produce effective leadership.

1. Trust your subordinates.

2. Develop a vision.

3. Keep your cool.

4. Encourage risk.

5. Be an expert.

6. Invite dissent.

7. Simplify.

These survey results do not add up to a neat package of "leadership qualities." They do, however, identify some traits and skills that are important components of leadership. The significant thing to be observed is that none of the traits is necessarily inborn. Leaders do not need to be born; they can be made.

Some managers are more effective than others. The more effective managers actively develop and use their power and influence. In addition to the power that goes along with their roles as managers, managers can increase their personal power. Developing interpersonal networks, using a pull rather than a push approach, and believing in the abilities of subordinates are all ways in which managers can become more effective leaders. Leadership is learnable. The qualities of leadership can be developed and nurtured. This conclusion is important for organizations as well as would-be leaders.

Selected Readings

Chapman, Elwood N. 1989. *Leadership: What Every Manager Needs to Know.* Chicago: Science Research Associates.

Jago, Arthur. 1982. "Leadership: Perspectives in Theory and Research." *Management Science.* 28 (3): 163–166.

Kanter, Rosabeth Moss. 1977. *Men and Women of the Corporation.* New York: Basic Books.

Kotter, John P. 1977. "Power, Dependence, and Effective Management." *Harvard Business Review* 55: 125–136.

Labich, Kenneth. 1988. "The Seven Keys to Business Leadership." *Fortune* (October 24): 58.

Lundy, Jim. 1986. *Lead, Follow, or Get Out of the Way.* San Diego: Avant Books.

McGregor, Douglas. 1960. *The Human Side of Enterprise.* New York: McGraw-Hill.

Mintzberg, Henry. 1983. *Power In and Around Organizations.* Englewood Cliffs, NJ: Prentice-Hall.

Salancik, G. R. and J. Pfeffer. 1977. "Who Gets Power—And How They Hold on to It: A Strategic-Contingency Model of Power." *Organizational Dynamics* 5: 3–21.

Smith, Kenwyn K., and David N. Berg. 1987. "A Paradoxical Conception of Group Dynamics." *Human Relations* 10: 633–657.

Yukl, Gary. 1981. *Leadership in Action.* Englewood Cliffs, NJ: Prentice-Hall.

Yukl, Gary, and Tom Taber. 1983. "The Effective Use of Managerial Power." *Personnel* 60: 37–44.

17

Leadership: Style, Situation, and Effectiveness

Managers are expensive. Their salaries and benefits are relatively high, and their training and development are costly. It may take years to develop in a manager the wisdom and the perspective necessary to do an effective job of leading.

As a result, organizations are very interested in finding the "right" people to train. What does a leader look like and act like? How can an organization spot leadership potential in a person early, so training and development efforts are expended wisely?

Questions like these have led managers and researchers alike to investigate leadership. This chapter presents a chronology of their findings.

TRAITS OF LEADERS

There is something intuitively appealing about the belief that leaders are special—that they were "born to lead" and so have a shared set of special traits. Probably the oldest leadership research was an attempt to identify those special shared traits. Some of the traits that have been investigated include intelligence, family income, social competence, personality, task focus, communications, education, and physical size.

Although there is some evidence that successful leaders score higher than average on a variety of traits, trait theory has not been predictive. For example, the ability to provide guidance and direction to coordinate subordinates' activities is a leadership trait found significantly more often in successful leaders than in unsuccessful leaders. However, possession of that ability would not be an accurate predictor of overall leadership ability.

The size theory provides another interesting example of trait research. It hypothesized that taller, more powerfully built people would be better leaders. Of course, actual data proved no correlation—some tall people are effective leaders; some are not. Some short people are effective leaders; some are not. A most interesting finding, however, comes from a recent study of 1200 male MBA graduates of the University of Pittsburgh. Graduates who were 6 feet tall earned an average of $4200 more than graduates 5 feet 5 inches. If the taller man was trim and the shorter man was at least 20 percent overweight, the wage difference increased to about $8200! Lack of evidence that size makes a difference in leadership ability has apparently not changed perceptions.

In general, trait theory is of limited value because it considers only the characteristics of the leader, and discounts the characteristics of the followers and the situation, all of which interact in a dynamic system. What good managers do in a variety of situations turned out to be more important than who they are.

BEHAVIORAL THEORIES

By the 1940s, researchers had turned their attention to identifying particular behaviors that might be characteristic of good leaders but not of weak ones. If such behaviors could be identified, then training efforts could be directed toward teaching them to would-be leaders. A number of major studies have investigated behavioral styles.

The Ohio State Studies

Begun in the 1940s, the Ohio State studies undertook a major investigation of leader behaviors. The researchers started with over 1000 behaviors which they hypothesized might influence leader effectiveness. They asked subordinates to indicate the extent to which they agreed with a wide variety of statements about the behaviors of their leaders. Ultimately, the list was narrowed to two independent dimensions.

1. *Initiating Consideration.* This dimension refers to the interpersonal skills of the leader. Does the leader indicate trust, respect, and regard for the feelings of subordinates? Leaders

who are high in consideration are friendly and approachable and will find time to listen to subordinates.

2. *Initiating Structure*. This dimension refers to the organizational and goal-achieving skills of the leader. Does the leader organize work well, assign tasks clearly, and have high work quality standards? Leaders who are high in initiating structure plan and schedule work, control closely, and set deadlines.

Because the dimensions are independent, a leader can be high on both, low on both, or high on one and low on the other. Follow-up research led to the conclusion that usually the leader who is high on both structural and consideration dimensions is perceived by subordinates to be the most effective. Some situations appear to influence what would be the most effective behaviors. For example, workers performing highly routine tasks do not like a manager with high structure-initiating behaviors. The job itself creates structure enough.

An important question which the Ohio State studies raise is, "are subordinates' perceptions of effective leadership the same as effective leadership from the organization's point of view?"

The University of Michigan Studies

Around the same time, researchers at the University of Michigan conducted a similar study into leadership behaviors. They also concentrated on two factors—employee orientation and production orientation. In the University of Michigan studies, subordinate perception was combined with an external measure of subordinate productivity. The studies concluded that an employee-oriented manager, one who focused on relationships rather than productivity, was in all cases better. The subordinates of such a manager were both more productive and more satisfied.

The Managerial Grid

Robert Blake and Jane Mouton continued studying these two dimensions, setting up laboratory experiments and collecting data from organizations. Their conclusion was that the manager who is high on both dimensions—concern for production and concern for people, is in all cases most effective. They now provide managerial training to help managers achieve that behavior goal. To assist in their training workshops, they constructed a 9 x 9 grid with "concern for production" on the horizontal axis and "concern for people" on the vertical axis. They specifically address five different leadership styles.

1,1 *Impoverished management*. This manager has little concern for either people or production.

9,1 *Authority-obedience*. The manager's focus is almost exclusively on production.

1,9 *Country club management*. The manager's concern is almost exclusively on relationships and getting along.

5,5 *Organization man management*. This manager is a compromiser and trades off production against morale.

9,9 *Team management*. This manager seeks high productivity by developing mutual trust and respect.

CONTINGENCY THEORIES

Like the trait theories of leadership, the behavioral theories seek a "one best way" of managing. Many researchers believe those explanations are too simplistic. They have produced models or theories that include a set of interacting factors which influence how subordinates will respond to certain managerial behavior. These research conclusions are referred to as contingency theories, because they hypothesize that the manager's best behavioral choice is contingent, or dependent, upon a variety of interrelated factors.

Fiedler's Contingency Model

Fred Fiedler, a researcher working in the 1960s, set out to identify a way of matching leader traits or behavior with the situations where the behavior would be most effective. In order to do so, he had to develop a measure of leader behaviors and a measure of situations.

LEAST PREFERRED CO-WORKER

In order to determine what sort of leader a particular person was, Fiedler asked managers to fill out a form which allowed them to describe their least preferred co-worker (LPC). High LPC scores indicate a manager has used positive terms to describe the least preferred co-worker. Low LPC scores indicate negative terms.

SITUATIONAL FACTORS

Fiedler identified three characteristics of the environment or situation that would affect the most effective leader behavior.

1. Leader-member relations—how well do the manager and the subordinates get along.

2. Task structure—how well structured, repetitive, and controlled are the tasks the subordinates are performing.

3. Leader position power—how much formal authority and ability to influence does the leader have.

From the leader's point of view, good member relations, a highly structured task, and high position power would make for the easiest or most favorable managing situation. Poor relationships with subordinates, an unstructured task, and low position power would be the most difficult or unfavorable situation. In both of these extreme cases, the task-oriented manager will do best. In those cases where conditions are moderately favorable, Fielder concluded that a relations-oriented style would be most effective.

Path-Goal Theory

Scholar Robert House related leadership to motivation. His Path-Goal Theory suggests that the best leaders will be those who show employees how their performance directly affects the rewards they will receive. House identified four managerial styles which he recommended managers adopt depending on the situation. The dimensions include direction, support, participation, and achievement orientation.

DIRECTION

A directive leader will tell the subordinate what to do and when to do it. The leader provides clear structure and firm control.

SUPPORT

The supportive leader shows an interest in employees, developing good interpersonal relationships with them. The leader is friendly and approachable.

PARTICIPATION

A highly participative manager involves employees in decision making—most frequently on issues that directly affect them and on other matters as well.

ACHIEVEMENT ORIENTATION

A leader whose style is high on achievement orientation sets challenging goals and supports followers in achieving them.

SITUATIONAL CHARACTERISTICS

According to Path-Goal Theory, two qualities of the environment would influence which behavioral dimensions a leader would choose.

1. Subordinate's characteristics. These include characteristics such as the subordinate's abilities, need for structure, acceptance of authoritarianism, and age.

2. Environmental factors. These include factors such as the nature of the task, organizational structure, the formal authority relationships, and informal groups.

Path-Goal Theory argues that subordinates will perceive each of the different leadership styles as acceptable, satisfying, and motivating in situations where they believe it is either an immediate source of desired personal goals or it is helpful in leading to desired goals.

Many researchers have used Path-Goal Theory to test hypotheses about leaders. Their findings are mixed. Usually, workers performing unstructured tasks prefer a more directive leader, while workers performing very structured tasks prefer a more supportive leader. Since the findings, however, are not universal, the most helpful contribution made by Path-Goal Theory is that the best leaders are flexible. They are sensitive to both the needs of subordinates and to the environmental context within which they manage.

Hersey and Blanchard's Situational Leadership

In 1982, with the data on contingency theories of leadership still offering mixed results, Paul Hersey and Kenneth Blanchard, scholars and management consultants, developed another situational leadership theory which practicing managers find helpful.

The key concept in their theory is the task-relevant readiness of the followers. Readiness is defined as the following.

1. Desire for achievement.

2. Willingness and ability to accept responsibility.

3. Education, experience, and skills necessary for the task.

This concept of readiness is combined with the historically helpful concepts of leader's task behavior and leader's relationship behavior to determine the most effective leadership style.

Hersey and Blanchard identified four different leadership styles based on four levels of worker readiness.

TELLING

When subordinates lack task readiness, the *telling* style is most appropriate. As a high-task, low-relationship style, the leader tells the subordinate what, how, when, and where to do the work. The telling leadership style would most likely be used with new employees who are just learning about the job and the organizational setting. When an organization introduces new technology, for example computers, a leader who has been using a different style might want to come back to a telling approach.

SELLING

The *selling* style is most appropriate for subordinates who are gaining a sense of their jobs, who have a good understanding of some tasks and perhaps poor understanding of other tasks. The selling style is both high on task-focused, directive behavior and high on relationship-focused, supportive behavior. The high- task behavior provides clarity for the employee still not ready for responsibility while the high-relationship behavior encourages and demonstrates trust and confidence.

PARTICIPATING

The *participating* style is appropriate in situations where the employee demonstrates high levels of task readiness. In the participating style, the leader reduces the number of task- focused behaviors. The employee will resent being closely directed. However, the leader retains a high relationship- behavior focus. In this way, the leader reinforces the employee's responsible task performance through a continued and developing personal relationship.

DELEGATING

When a follower has reached the highest level of task readiness, the *delegating* style is most appropriate. Achieving this high level of task readiness implies the follower has both the ability to complete the tasks at a high degree of expertise, and also has the internal motivation. When subordinates fall into this category, a low-task, low-relationship leadership style is most appropriate.

Hersey and Blanchard's model provides a helpful framework for thinking about the situational variables that influence appropriate leadership styles. The model makes it clear that effective leadership behaviors are situationally determined. Flexibility and adaptability are required qualities of the best leaders. As follower readiness varies over time, the effective leader's focus adapts to the changes.

Hersey and Blanchard's model also helps explain why some managers are terrific in one setting and not so good in another. If a supervisor who spends most of his or her time training new employees develops a telling, highly directive, task-focused style, that supervisor will most likely be very effective. However, if the manager is promoted and now manages experienced, motivated employees using the previously successful telling style, leadership effectiveness will drop. Subordinates will feel "bossed around." They are likely to become less responsible and less motivated. Leaders must adapt their behaviors to the situation.

Vroom and Yetton's Decision- Making Model

Several chapters ago, decision making was identified as a core managerial function—what managers do. There are a variety of ways, however, for a manager to go about decision making, Victor Vroom and Philip Yetton focused their 1970s leadership research on identifying situational variables that have impact specifically on the manager's decision-making style.

A manager can involve subordinates in the decision-making process to different degrees. Vroom and Yetton concluded that the following elements influence how involved subordinates should be in the decision-making process.

1. The quality or rationality of the decision
2. The acceptance or commitment of the subordinates to the decision
3. The amount of time allowed for making the decision
4. The leader's knowledge/expertise
5. The degree of concensus likely among subordinates

They concluded that five different decision-making styles would be appropriate in different situations. The different styles are as follows.

ALTERNATIVE DECISION-MAKING STYLES

The Level I, Autocratic decision type (AI) is the most autocratic. The leader makes the decision based on information at hand.

The Level II, Autocratic style (AII) is also autocratic—the leader makes the decision. The difference is that the leader obtains information from subordinates first.

Level I, Consultative (CI) is a consultative style—the leader shares the problem with some subordinates independently and seeks their ideas. Then the leader makes the decision.

The Level II, Consultative (CII) style suggests that the leader get subordinates together in a group, shares the problem, and seeks suggestions. The leader then makes a decision independently.

Level II, Group (GII) is a group decision-making style. The problem is shared with the group. Together, alternatives are generated and a consensus agreement is reached. The manager using this decision-making style acts more as a group chairperson who accepts the group's decision.

PERSONAL STYLE

Even though research provides evidence that certain leadership behaviors work best in certain situations, a manager's personal style and perceptual set are important as well. Each manager looks at the world through a filter of values, beliefs, and prejudices. As McGregor's Theory X and Theory Y assumptions point out, a manager is not a computer who acts rapidly and rationally. The more out-of-character managers act, the more energy they must expend and the less competent they become. Stress (for both leader and follower) results. So the conclusions of situational leadership must be tempered with an acceptance of personal style.

TRANSFORMATIONAL LEADERSHIP

A group of management theorists and consultants are taking a new look at leadership. Based on the work of Abraham Maslow, Elizabeth Kübler-Ross, Fritz Perls, Virginia Satir, and others of the human potential movement of the 1960s and 1970s, transformational leadership assists organizations and their members to become more than they thought they could be—to become "transformed."

Bernard Bass, a researcher working with the U.S. Army, set out a clear distinction between transactional leaders and transformational leaders.

Transactional Leadership

Transactional leadership is what traditional scholars mean when they refer to leaders and managers. According to Bass, *transactional* leadership is an exchange process. Followers' needs are met when they perform according to their contracts with the leader. The transactional leader:

1. Recognizes what actions subordinates must take to achieve organizational goals,

2. Clarifies the actions,

3. Recognizes subordinates' needs,

4. Clarifies the connection between subordinate actions and needs.

Transformational Leadership

The *transformational* leader approaches leadership from an entirely different perspective or level of awareness. Rather than better application of the same principles, as proposed by the contingency theorists, improvement comes from the application of different principles. According to Bass, the transformational leader:

1. Raises levels of consciousness about the importance of certain goals or actions,

2. Encourages subordinates to transcend self-interests for the good of the team,

3. Causes subordinates to focus on higher-order needs such as self-actualization.

Gandhi's leadership of India in its struggle against Britain for self-rule is cited as an example of transformational leadership. He asked that followers abandon their use of active aggression, and instead apply passive resistance. He asked that they transcend personal fear and focus on the shared goal of an independent India. Through his own behavior, Gandhi served as a model, which he encouraged followers to adopt.

Gandhi focused on changing the culture rather than on controlling the behavior of individual members of the culture. Transformational leadership proponents assert that the real role of a leader is to manage organizational culture. If a leader focuses all of his or her managerial attention on controlling the behavior of individuals, the organization will remain where it is. If, alternatively, the leader focuses on developing an organizational culture that supports the creativity and personal and professional growth of its members, the organization becomes self-controlling. The leader is freed to identify opportunities and challenges in the larger environment. The result in terms of organizational performance is exponential. Chapter 24 will discuss this topic further.

Robert House, who developed Path-Goal Theory in the 1970s, has moved into the study of transformational leadership. He reviewed sociological and political literature to isolate what he believes to be qualities of the transformational leader. Sometimes referred to as *charismatics*, these leaders:

1. *Serve as role model.* They express through their actions a set of values and beliefs which followers imitate or adopt.

2. *Build an image.* They take actions which are consciously designed to build their image in the eyes of the followers.

3. *Articulate goals.* They communicate "transcendent" goals which become the basis of the group's "cause."

4. *Set high expectations.* They indicate not only high standards but also confidence in the followers' ability to reach them.

Those researchers and consultants who are studying transformational leadership claim that major change at the cultural or organizational level *requires* transformational leadership. Global concerns over the health of the environment, peace, and population growth, and organizational responses to technological and demographic changes are imperatives which demand major changes or shifts in how work is accomplished. If the transformational leadership investigators are correct, leaders will need to develop new skills. Richard Byrd has identified five skills which he believes future leaders must have.

1. *Anticipatory skills*—the ability to both intuitively and systematically scan the environment for meaningful changes.

2. *Visioning skills*—the ability to articulate vision and motivate action toward it.

3. *Value-congruence skills*—understanding follower needs and developing an organizational culture of shared motives, values, and goals.

4. *Empowerment skills*—the ability to share power with others.

5. *Self-understanding skills*—the ability to be introspective and act congruently.

Transformational leadership develops an organizational culture which values the spiritual essence of people. As a result, traditional research methodologies do not provide a framework for its systematic investigation, making the topic somewhat suspect. The growing application of the principles of quantum mechanics to fields other than physics may soon provide the necessary framework, however. Fritjof Capra's *The Tao of Physics* and Deepak Chopra's *Quantum Healing* provide examples of the growing incorporation of spirituality into "hard sciences." This interesting topic will undoubtedly be increasingly addressed by management scholars and practitioners.

Leadership research leads to the conclusions that leadership behavior is more important than leader traits, and that effective behaviors are a function of situation. Any leadership situation includes specific qualities of the subordinates, of the leader, and of the context, all of which have impact.

In general, a leader's job is to help followers complete the work of the organization. As Path-Goal Theory puts it, leaders need to show followers how the accomplishment of organizational work will result in the achievement of personal as well as organizational goals.

As previous chapters have pointed out, individual goals as well as individual ability and motivation change over time. The excellent leader recognizes the changes and chooses different paths on different days. The transformational leader sees a new level of potential in organizations by helping followers achieve more of their self-actualization and spiritual goals.

SELECTED READINGS

Bass, Bernard. 1985. "Leadership: Good, Better, Best." *Organizational Dynamics* 13: 26–40.

Blake, Robert, and Jane Mouton. 1978. *The New Managerial Grid*. Houston: Gulf Publishing.

Byrd, Richard E. 1987. "Corporate Leadership Skills: A New Synthesis." *Organizational Dynamics* 16: 31–40.

Fiedler, Fred E. 1967. *A Theory of Leadership Effectiveness*. New York: McGraw-Hill.

Graeff, C. L. 1983. "The Situational Leadership Theory: A Critical View." *Academy of Management Review* 8: 285–291.

Hersey, Paul, and Kenneth Blanchard. 1982. *Management of Organizational Behavior*, 4th ed. Englewood Cliffs, NJ: Prentice Hall.

House, Robert. 1971. "A Path-Goal Theory of Leadership Effectiveness." *Administrative Science Quarterly* 16: 321–338.

House, Robert. 1977. "A 1976 Theory of Charismatic Leadership." in *Leadership: The Cutting Edge*, edited by J. G. Hunt and L. L. Larson. Carbondale, IL: Southern Illinois University Press.

Likert, Rensis. 1967. *The Human Organization*. New York: McGraw-Hill.

McGregor, Douglas. 1961. *The Human Side of Enterprise*. New York: McGraw-Hill.

Pascale, Richard T., and Anthony G. Athos. 1981. *The Art of Japanese Management: Applications for American Executives*. New York: Simon and Schuster.

Stogdill, Ralph M. 1948. "Personal Factors Associated with Leadership: A Survey of the Literature." *Journal of Psychology* 25: 35–71.

Stogdill, R. M., and A. E. Coons, eds. 1951. *Leader Behavior: Its Description and Measurement*. Monograph 88, Columbus, OH: Ohio State University.

Tichy, N. M., and D. O. Ulrich. 1984. "The Leadership Challenge—A Call for the Transformational Leader." *Sloan Management Review* Fall: 59–68.

Vroom, Victor, and Philip Yetton. 1973. *Leadership and Decision Making*. Pittsburgh, PA: University of Pittsburgh Press.

18

Communication

If decision making is the core managerial function, then communication is the core managerial skill. Some would claim that managing is the same as communicating. In fact, in their book, In Search of Excellence: Lessons from America's Best-Run Companies, Thomas Peters and Robert Waterman concluded that excellent companies are very different from nonexcellent companies specifically in the way their members communicate.

Because reading and writing, listening and speaking are skills, they can be learned. Every manager and would-be manager will be more effective as these communication skills are developed.

The quality of communication is affected not only by the skill of the communicators, but also by the structure or channels within which it occurs. Organizations have control over their communication structures. In this chapter, the various functions of and structures for transmitting communication will be discussed.

THE COMMUNICATION PROCESS

Communication is the transfer of information, ideas, understanding, or feelings. Managing is "working with and through others," and communication is necessary so that each knows his or her role in the process of accomplishing the work.

Communication is almost infinitely complex—messages are being simultaneously sent and received through all the body's sensing mechanisms. In spite of the complexity of actual communication, a highly sim-

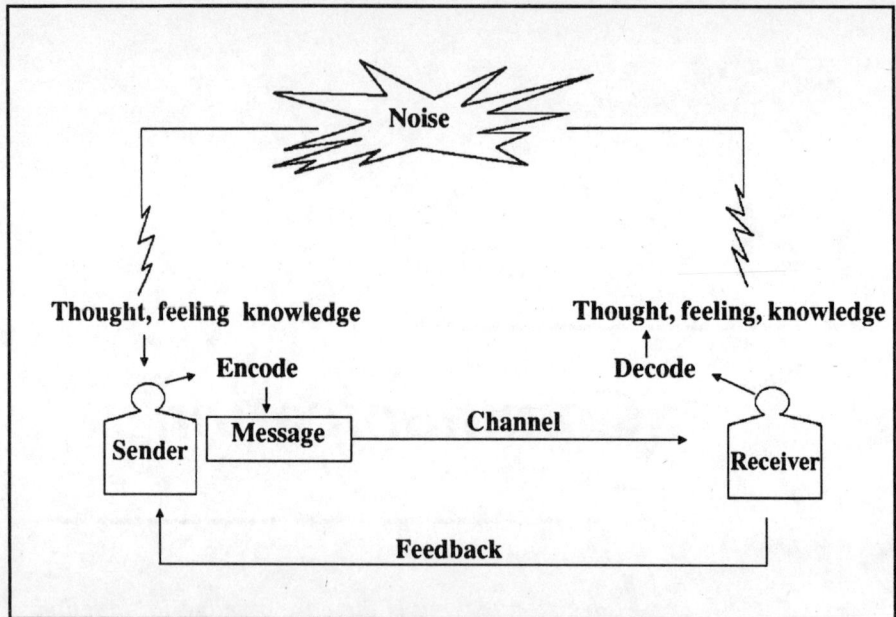

Fig. 18.1 Simplified Communication Model

plified model of the communication process provides a framework for talking about communication—what can go wrong and what to consider in making communication effective.

The communication process begins when a sender wants to communicate something. The message has meaning for the sender, but an encoding process must occur before the meaning can be sent or transmitted to another, the receiver. *Encoding* means translating the thought or feeling which is internal to the sender into a code which can be transmitted. The code might be for example, spoken words, written math symbols, or body movement. The sender then chooses a *channel*, the actual medium by which the message will be sent. Example of channels include the telephone, a face-to-face meeting, or a written memo.

When the receiver gets the communication, it must be *decoded*—taken out of symbol code and translated back into thought or feeling meaning. Once a message or meaning has been decoded, the receiver will most likely return a message. This part of the process is called *feedback*. Although this simple model implies that communication is one-way, actual communication is simultaneous and multidimensional. A sender might send a message, "Barney, will you please come in my office," using an aural channel. At the exact time that the message is being sent, Barney might be sending his own nonverbal message by looking up from his desk and smiling.

At any stage in the process, something can interfere with the effectiveness, clarity, or accuracy of the communication. This interference is called *noise*. Noise can be physical, such as a lawn mower outside the window; psychological, such as fear or anxiety; the result of faulty transmission, as when the telephone line goes dead; or anything else that keeps the message from being accurately received.

The communication process takes place in a context or background. Some elements of the context are structural and some are psychological. Examples of the psychological environment might include how tired the communicators are or their relative status in the organization. Structural elements of the context might include whether the communication takes place in a formal business meeting or at the drinking fountain. The context also influences how effective, clear, or accurate the communication is.

BARRIERS TO COMMUNICATION

Most people's personal experience is that it is easier to miscommunicate than to communicate clearly. Understanding some of the more common reasons for miscommunication is helpful in improving the quality of communication.

Physical Interference

The first step in improving communication is to make sure the receiver received a message. Telephone answering machines do not always work, mail is occasionally misdirected, police sirens go off during conversations, machinery makes noise. Additionally, twenty million people in the U. S. have impaired hearing and another twenty million people cannot read.

The sender must assume responsibility for seeing that the physical barriers to communication are reduced. Moving to a quieter room, making eye contact, sending a followup memo, considering the receiver's ability to read, and turning off the television are all ways communicators can take control of the physical environment and reduce physical interference.

Psychological Noise

When the receiver is distracted, thinking about something else, the message may not be received accurately. Workers anxious about potential layoffs may not decode a message on retirement benefits the way the author intended. Hunger, anger, and joy may each have a different impact on what the receiver understands. For example, studies show that students, being given a list of criticisms about their work, hear no more than the first three. Fourth, fifth, sixth criticisms are blocked by a brain thinking up defenses or handling embarrassment or anger. The expression "food for thought" will strike a hungry listener differently from someone who has just overeaten.

Asking for feedback, providing feedback, and verifying the accuracy of the decoded message helps greatly in identifying psychological barriers.

Information Processing Problems

Although the brain works literally at lightening speed, it can process consciously only one thought at a time. As a result, when information comes too fast or there is too much of it, the brain has trouble "getting it." Witnesses' reports of accidents substantiate this. Different witnesses process different aspects of the incident. A video tape of the accident scene might indicate that all the witnesses were correct, they just were not complete.

PATTERN RECOGNITION

One information processing problem paradoxically arises because the brain is excellent at pattern recognition. As a result, the brain will take incomplete information and attribute patterned meaning to it. For example, if it is typical for written assignments to be due on Fridays in a particular class, students are likely to "mishear" if the instructor sets Wednesday as the due date for one assignment because they do not expect that part of the pattern to change. They will listen to the content requirements because they expect those to change. As research has demonstrated, people perceive what they expect to perceive. Identifying patterns or groups in information allows the brain to make sense of data rapidly. It can also lead to miscommunication if the information being transmitted is not part of a usual pattern.

RECENCY EFFECT

Individuals also tend to give more credence and emphasis to the most recent information. This is called the *recency effect*. For example, when a subordinate's performance is being evaluated, the most recent boss/subordinate interaction is likely to be given the most attention. If, during the first three quarters of the year, an employee's performance was above standard, and the last quarter performance was significantly below standard, the employee is likely to receive a poor evaluation. Alternatively, three poor quarters followed by a very strong quarter are likely to result in an overall positive evaluation. The meaning a receiver makes of information depends partly on the order in which the information is received.

COMMUNICATION OVERLOAD

Communication overload refers to situations where so much information is transmitted that the receiver cannot process it all. Computerized data banks sometimes provide so much information that none of it is used. The receiver of the information becomes overwhelmed and shuts down the receiving process. One of the most important functions of information systems managers is to control the amount of information provided to members of an organization. Too much information results in poorer quality decisions than if not enough information is present.

Perceptual Factors

People experience communication from an egocentric perspective. They put themselves in the central position. That perceptual bias leads to statements like the following, collected by the BOLA Society of Arizona from an automobile accident report: "The tree swerved into my path and I hit it."

Egocentrism can also lead to communication breakdown, especially when the sender's language lacks specificity. For example, if a sender says "too many employees are taking more than an hour for lunch," the egocentric receiver will hear "you are taking more than an hour for lunch," and will become defensive. Greater language specificity will reduce this barrier. For example, "Bob and SueEllen took a two-hour lunch on Thursday" is a more clearly specific way to communicate the information.

Each individual also brings a unique set of past experiences to a communication. These experiences affect the meaning communicators attach to message symbols. For example, an employee who has experienced being laid off will most likely read the company policy on seniority differently than an employee who has never faced that trauma.

An employee's cultural roots are a major part of his or her background. As a result, cultural differences may influence the quality of communication significantly. When Americans are asked to wait thirty minutes for an appointment, they are likely to feel that the other does not value them and believes them to be of lower status. As a result, they will probably enter the communication feeling hostile or defensive. They will tend to look for more information that verifies their perception.

In Mexico and other Latin American countries, waiting does not convey status. A Mexican who takes thirty minutes to receive a visitor would be considered neither rude nor status conscious.

Power Issues

Although both experience and research demonstrate that employees need information in order to work efficiently and effectively, information is frequently withheld. The reason is that possessing knowledge that others need gives one power. "Information brokers" receive a great deal of attention. One way to overcome this barrier is to realize that shared knowledge expands everyone's power. Knowledge held too closely has the long-term result of shutting the information broker out of the knowledge network. Once co-workers discover a worker who clings to important information that would make their work easier, they begin to go around that person, both to acquire and to share information.

STRUCTURAL BARRIERS

Some aspects of organization structure can affect the quality of communication. Because communication is so vital to the smooth functioning of a group, organizations consider communication issues when designing organizational structure.

Links in the Chain

The greater the number of people in a chain of communicators, the greater the likelihood that message distortion will result. A game played by school children called Gossip illustrates this structural communication barrier well. A message is passed in whispers from person to person throughout a group. The last person to receive the message says it out loud. The person who began the message announces what the message originally was. If the communication chain has over ten "links," the chances are excellent that the final message will be substantially different from the initial message. Positives are switched to negatives, and names and days of the week are changed—the important details become confused.

In addition to reduced payrolls, organizations that cut or lower their management levels find they reap the additional reward of improved communication.

Status

People communicate more easily with people on the same hierarchical level. Differences in status or hierarchical level may result in poor quality communication because of a process called *information filtering*. Subordinates tend to "soften" bad news when communicating with their bosses. They phrase the bad news in more positive terms, perhaps omitting some of it altogether.

When bosses communicate downward, they tend to filter out much of what they know, passing on only a relatively small amount. When questioned about their communication strategy, they tend to reply that more information would only confuse their subordinates and that it is not relevant. They firmly believe that they have passed on all the necessary information. Interestingly, study after study indicates that subordinates at every organizational level wish their bosses would share more information with them.

Overcoming the communication barriers imposed by status differences is mostly a matter of realizing they are likely to occur. Seeking and providing feedback and verifying information will help. So will reducing the symbols of differential status—reserved parking spaces, special restrooms, private club membership, and so on.

Limited Sources

When a communicator must rely on only one source for information, the chances go up that the information will be filtered. For example, untrue negative information spreads rapidly in situations where no one has the information to demonstrate the fallacy of it. Having multiple sources of information and verifying the content of a communication serve as the most effective strategies for overcoming this barrier.

Lack of Trust

Lack of trust can be a major barrier to clear and accurate communication. Usually people think of lack of trust and openness as an interpersonal problem. It can, however, be an organizationwide problem. When managers send the message that their orders are not to be questioned, that they are not interested in hearing about ways to improve the work process, or that they do not want to hear "excuses," they set up a hostile communication climate. When an organization controls and supervises too closely, real communication decreases and information filtering increases.

Time and Workload Pressures

Stress reduces an individual's ability to communicate with clarity and accuracy. When an organization demands too much of its employees in too little time, employees' stress levels increase and their ability to communicate declines. Thoughtful work analysis and job design can reduce time and workload pressures and improve communication.

COMMUNICATION CHANNELS

In an organization, communication can be either formal—following the hierarchy planned during organizational design, or informal—part of the informal group process. The path a communication takes through an organization has an effect upon the communication.

Formal Communication

A communication that follows the hierarchy of reporting relationships in an organization is referred to as *formal* communication. Such a communication can flow from the bottom hierarchical level upward, or from a higher level downward. Organizations communicate in each direction in somewhat universal ways.

DOWNWARD FORMAL COMMUNICATION

The most frequently used formal channel of communication for any individual employee is the chain of command, that series of authority or reporting relationships which starts with the president or top manager. The most common way messages are transmitted downward along the chain of command is through face-to-face interactions. Because formal downward communication carries information about what job to do, how to do it, and when it is to be completed, good listening skills are important survival skills for subordinates.

Organizations also communicate downward through written documents. In addition to a variety of memoranda, some of the typical methods include pay inserts—messages included with a worker's check; the house organ—a company's internally distributed newsletter; bulletin boards—regular places where company news is posted; and employee handbooks—the company's policies and procedures, especially as they relate to employee benefits and employee responsibilities.

UPWARD FORMAL COMMUNICATION

All organizations have provisions for communicating formally with employees in a downward direction. In the past, U. S. organizations believed informal channels would be sufficient for carrying news upward. However, a growing number of organizations are establishing formal ways for employees to communicate upward. The result is more accurate managerial decision-making information and greater employee participation in the management and control of the organization. Formal upward channels of communication were one of the qualities of the best-run companies that Peters and Waterman identified in *In Search of Excellence*.

Some widely used methods for formal upward communication include the suggestion box—a system which guarantees that an employee's ideas will be carefully considered; grievance procedures—a systematic process which employees can use to complain about matters affecting them personally; ombudsperson—an individual who will confidentially hear employee complaints, investigate, and make recommendations to management; anonymous questionnaires—surveys of employee attitudes and levels of satisfaction; and special meetings—meetings where the agenda is to receive employee feedback on any number of issues from new policies to product design to work methods.

Informal Communication

As was discussed in chapter 15, organizations are actually interlinked groups, many of which are informal. Informal communication in the organization reflects the cross linking of small groups. Managers of different departments get together over lunch to discuss a policy that affects them both (lateral communication.) An employee who is having boss/subordinate trouble asks a friend of the boss to intercede (diagonal communication.)

The informal communication network is referred to as the *grapevine*. The most significant feature of informal communication is that it is based on mutual trust. The grapevine has four basic characteristics.

1. It transmits information in all directions. Messages can flow up, down, laterally, and diagonally.

2. It transmits information simultaneously, so it is very fast. The growth in voice-mail and electronic-mail systems has made the grapevine even faster.

3. It is selective with regard to who receives information. Because informal communication is trust-based, those who are not trusted are not included. It is possible for an organizational member to be completely unaware that a grapevine exists.

4. It extends beyond the boundaries of the organization. Spouses and friends in other companies are frequently included. The informal communication network in an organization is composed of clusters of relationships. An organization's grapevine then becomes a cluster in a larger external grapevine.

IMPROVING COMMUNICATION EFFECTIVENESS

In addition to becoming aware of the typical barriers to effective communication, individual managers can take additional steps to improve their personal communication competence. The following suggestions involve a change in attitude. When a communicator approaches a communication interaction with a different attitude, more effective communication behaviors will automatically result.

Avoid Judgment

The interpersonal communication literature stresses that avoiding judgment and evaluation is the single most important ingredient in truly effective communication. If the emphasis is instead placed on accurate and specific *description*, defensiveness is reduced and trust is increased. The communicators can "put down their guard" and listen more carefully.

As an example, compare the likely results of the following two statements.

1. "Your constant tardiness is clear evidence that you are not happy working for this company. What do you have to say for yourself?"

2. "You were ten minutes late on Monday, 22 minutes late on Tuesday, and seven minutes late today. I would like to discuss this with you."

The judgmental tone of the first statement will make it difficult for the first subordinate to share relevant information.

Avoid Certainty

Five words are almost automatic triggers to poor communication. They are ones that indicate certainty—that the communicator has all the answers. The words are "always," "never," "know," "sure," and "certain."

Rather than approaching communication with an attitude of certainty, the effective communicator takes a "wait and see" attitude. He or she gathers information and remembers that the brain's pattern recognition facility may encourage it to reach conclusions too rapidly.

Value Others

In a number of both subtle and obvious ways, people indicate their attitudes toward others. When a communicator indicates that others are valuable, the others are more willing to share information. Communication is then enhanced.

Indicating others' value can be accomplished in a number of ways. One is to avoid controlling others. Taking a problem-solving approach to differences, looking for a win-win solution rather than an "I win" solution, will indicate that what happens to others is as important as what happens to the self.

Another way to indicate the value of others is to recognize that all organizational members have a point of view to share. No one view is the superior view. Rather than superiority, the effective communicator brings an attitude of equality to communication interactions. Most communicators have more trouble valuing some people than others. Some common superiority/inferiority biases include listening to people significantly older, significantly younger, less well educated, of a different race, with whom there is strong competition, of a different sex, or of a different religion.

An additional way to indicate others' value is to empathize with them. *Empathy* is trying to see the world through the other person's eyes. When a communicator practices empathy, the other becomes real and more central. The alternative to empathy is impersonality. For generations, organizations have sought to reach the goal of impersonalization with employees. The result frequently is employee burn-out and high turnover. The way to improved organizational and communicational effectiveness is to value the uniqueness of individuals—to have empathy with them.

CURRENT TOPICS IN ORGANIZATIONAL COMMUNICATION

As technology makes communication faster, easier, and more global in its reach, researchers are becoming increasingly interested in studying human communication systems. Some of the topics which are especially interesting to managers include the following.

Intrapersonal Communication

As S. Helmstetter claims in his book *The Self-Talk Solution*, what communicators say to themselves turns out to be very important. The body manufactures hormones which reflect the communication the mind is having with itself. For example, if the internal dialog says, "I am so tired I don't know what I'm going to do. I just can't get that project started today," the brain will produce hormones that make the muscles feel tired and stiff. The production and distribution of these chemicals can take less than a second.

New research is discovering the power of self-talk or intrapersonal communication in creating the reality a person experiences. This field of research is growing rapidly.

Nonverbal Communication

Researchers have noted that in face-to-face interactions, as much as 93 percent of a message is transmitted nonverbally, through voice speed, volume, and tone, through body language, through the use of time and space. Cataloging nonverbal cues, however, has been difficult. A certain movement of the hand might be interpreted one way in one context and another way in another context. Recent medical research may explain why.

New findings indicate that humans produce pheromones in response to their emotions. *Pheromones* are hormone-like chemicals that the skin releases into the air. In minute concentrations, the skin of others picks up the emotional message. When someone says, "the air was thick with anxiety" or "the whole house seemed filled with sadness," those expressions are turning out to be literally true. Via the pheromones, communicators receive powerful nonverbal messages which may or may not be correlated with verbal or body languages. Scholars of communication now have an entire new field of research to explore.

Media Relations

Another growing communication field is public or media relations. An organization's relationship with its suppliers, customers, and employees is increasingly impacted by the image the organization has in the media. As a result, companies are becoming "media smart." They are learning about image management and public relations. Because managers represent their companies to the public, they must add effective media relations to their job skills.

In an animal, blood serves to connect the various cells and body systems into a functioning organism. In an organization, communication is the lifeline which connects each individual and group into a functioning whole. Quality communication is essential.

Communication can be thought of as a flow of information. However, psychological, physical, and structural barriers can cause turbulence in the information flow. Effective managers work to reduce the barriers. The more rapidly and reliably they receive information, the better quality decisions they can make. In addition to improving the basic skills of communication—reading, writing, listening, and speaking, managers can improve their communication effectiveness by withholding judgment, avoiding certainty, and valuing others.

Selected Readings

Anderson, Joyce S. 1989. "Real Open-Door Communication." *Personnel Journal* 68: 32–37.

Davis, Keith. 1969. "Grapevine Communication Among Lower and Middle Managers." *Personnel Journal* (April): 269–272.

Lengel, Robert H., and Richard L. Daft. 1988. "The Selection of Communication Media as an Executive Skill." *Academy of Management Executive* 2: 225–234.

Mehrabian, Albert. 1971. *Silent Messages*. Belmont, CA: Wadsworth Publishing.

Nelton, Sharon. 1986. "Beyond Body Language." *Nation's Business* (June): 73–74.

Peters, T. J., and R. H. Waterman. 1982. *In Search of Excellence: Lessons from America's Best-Run Companies*. New York: Harper & Row.

Raney, Austin. 1983. *Channels of Power*. New York: Basic Books.

Ruch, R. V. 1984. *Corporate Communications: A Comparison of Japanese and American Practices*. Westport, CT: Quorum Books.

Staw, B., and L. L. Cummings, eds. 1984. *Research in Organizational Behavior*. Greenwich, CT: JAI Press.

Zarembra, Alan. 1989. "Communicating Upward." *Personnel Journal* 68: 34–39.

19

Control

Controlling is a process of comparing actual performance with performance standards and taking corrective action if necessary. As the chapters on planning discussed, setting standards is part of planning. Fundamentally, planning helps an organization decide what path to take. Controlling helps an organization stay on the path.

Each day is filled with crises and opportunities. Without an effective control process, an organization would wander around, responding to daily exigencies. The control process provides important feedback about where an organization is and what changes in direction are required. Control helps everyone keep to the path.

THE CONTROL PROCESS

The student of management, reading a book that addresses each of the functional areas of management independently, may, by the nineteenth chapter, begin to feel that the job of managing comes in individual, block-like chunks. Of course, each of the functional areas of management is actually a subsystem which interacts dynamically with the other functional subsystems. This fact is particularly important to recall when the topic of control is addressed. Nearly every step in the control process is directly affected by or directly affects the other functional processes.

The control process is part of the planning process. The goals or objectives established as the outcome of planning become the standards used in controlling. Feedback from the control process influences the standards set in the next planning cycle.

Controls influence employee motivation. When feedback from the control system is timely and constructive, motivation is increased. When controls are restrictive or feedback arrives too late for employees to take corrective action, motivation will decline.

The human resource management functions of employee selection, training, and evaluation are part of the process of controlling labor quality. Employee absenteeism and turnover may be signs of a poor control process. As a result of all the dynamic interactions between the controlling function and other managerial functions, the control process is very important.

Elements of the Control Process

Controlling involves comparing actual performance with standard expectations, and taking corrective action where necessary. In order to accomplish this goal, a control process must include several elements.

1. *Standards*. As mentioned already, standards are set as part of planning. They are essentially the result or outcome of operations planning. An example of a standard is "2.1 labor hours per unit produced." Wages, product selling price, size of workforce, and other factors are related to this planned standard of worker efficiency.

2. *Monitoring systems*. The organization must have established methods for measuring actual output. Developing the case above, the total number of units produced and the total number of labor hours must be counted for a particular time period.

3. *Evaluating systems*. Some method of evaluation or interpretation must be applied to the output measures to decide if they are close enough to standard or if they require correction. Suppose that 62 units were produced and 134 labor hours were used. That's just over 2.16 hours per unit. The evaluating system would decide whether the difference between 2.16 hours and 2.1 hours is significant and requires correcting.

4. *Feedback systems*. Information that results from the evaluation will help an organization take corrective action only if it gets where it can do the most good, and gets there in a timely fashion. Managers, workers, and planners each need some version of feedback. If the workers are told that productivity is dropping, they might be able to adjust rapidly.

Or on the other hand, perhaps several machines are broken down, and management needs to consider replacing them.

5. *Corrective actions*. When actual and standard are determined to be significantly different from one another, corrective action is called for. Some organizations focus on symptom alleviation. Other organizations seek to correct causative problems. Renting additional machines while the company's machines are repaired will help with the symptom of lower labor productivity. Determining why the machines are breaking down might provide a longer term solution. Perhaps maintenance is not performed, or no time for maintenance was figured into the labor productivity standard.

6. *Reward systems*. Desired behavior which is desired will be repeated when it is rewarded. Reward systems that are linked with the control process are most effective. If employees receive a share of profits, research indicates they take more pride and "ownership" of the production process.

Proactive Control

An ideal control process is proactive rather than reactive. That means it is designed to prevent problems—to keep the system on course—rather than to catch and correct problems which have already been made. An example of proactive control, common among Japanese firms and growing among U. S. firms, is the practice of sending a company employee to work with the quality control technicians at a supplier's factory. In other words, if Interstate Batteries buys its plastic battery cases from a supplier that manufactures molded plastic items, Interstate might pay a plastics engineer to work with the supplier to guarantee quality raw materials for Interstate's final product.

WHAT TO MEASURE: THE STANDARDS

As Harold S. Hook is famous for saying, "A company gets what it inspects, not what it expects." The setting of standards typically has powerful behavioral consequences. Motivation research has determined that standards that motivate share certain characteristics.

1. Standards must be objective. Another way of saying this is that they are measurable and can be applied impersonally. University faculty members are frequently evaluated on the "significance" of their research. Significance is a subjective, not objective, standard. As a result, debates over what

constitutes significance are typical on university campuses. Some schools have attempted to make the quality of significance more measurable by looking at "how many times a faculty member's research has been referenced in other researchers' work."

In production settings, objective measures are relatively easy to set and use—number of useable parts produced per shift, for example. Objective measures for service and information workers are more difficult to set. "New car sales" is an objective measure for car salespeople. A better measure might be "new car sales to repeat customers," because it would be a broader indicator of good customer service. The problem with that as a standard, however, is its long time frame.

2. For standards to motivate, they must be timely. People prefer frequent feedback. They like to know how they are doing as they go along. When they find out at the end of the year that their performance was not up to standard, there is nothing they can do about it. Working to standard becomes less important in situations with little or delayed feedback.

Americans are frequently criticized for their focus on the short run. The focus is the result of short-term goals, and the short-term goals are the result of evidence that short-term goals have greater motivational impact. The problem is self-generating.

3. In order for a standard to be motivational, the individual must be able to influence its achievement. When a project is not under a worker's control, being held responsible for it is frustrating and demotivating. As the discussion of delegation addressed, authority is a necessary part of responsibility.

4. Standards that are motivating are complete and inclusive. When employees are expected to turn out a high-quality product or service and are only rewarded for turning out high quantity, they soon lose their motivation to pay attention to quality.

Types of Standards

There are a number of common types of standards. For many of them, control tolerances are stated along with the standard. *Control tolerances* specify how much deviation from standard will be allowed before corrective action will be taken. For example, glass for 8" x 10" picture frames may be $8'' \pm .10'' \times 10'' \pm .15''$. The frame manufacturing process can accommodate that much variation. More variation than that, and the frame maker will reject the glass order. Types of standards, each of which might have a control tolerance, include the following.

1. *Time standards.* These standards establish how long something should take to make or to do. Domino's Pizza says they will deliver a pizza in 30 minutes. When a service writer prepares an auto repair estimate, the estimate is based on standard or average time allowances. These standard times are industry averages, published for use by all auto repair facilities.

2. *Production standards.* These standards specify output per unit of time. A garment worker is expected to complete the sewing of 8 shirts per shift. An insurance salesperson is expected to sell $100,000 in policies per month. Merck, a pharmaceutical company, expects sales representatives to contact a set number of doctors per month.

3. *Quality standards.* These standards set levels of performance and perfection. For example, AT&T telephones must be able to survive a 12-foot drop and work reliably.

   The U. S. Department of Commerce awards an annual Baldrige Award for Quality to a U. S. company for its attention to quality. According to Curt Reiman, administrator of the Baldrige, the award is based on three key areas: (1) customer satisfaction; (2) product and service quality; and (3) quality of internal operations. (*Fortune*, August 26, 1991, p. 34.)

4. *Cost standards.* These standards are commonly found in the budget. They set expected dollar costs. Cost standards might be set for raw materials or electrical power. Safeway grocery store managers are given monthly labor cost standards by corporate headquarters.

5. *Behavioral standards.* These standards apply to individuals and their behavior. For example all male workers at Disney-Land and DisneyWorld must be clean shaven—no beards or mustaches are allowed. Many companies do not allow employees to chew gum or smoke when interacting with customers. Most cities require that their fire and police department employees live within the city limits. Most workers are willing to follow behavioral standards while at work. When the behavioral standards extend into their off-work time, more resistance is encountered.

WHEN TO MEASURE: PROCESS CONTROL

The earlier in the production process a problem is identified, the better. Reworking is an expensive method of maintaining quality. As W. Edwards Deming, the famous consultant to Japanese manufacturers, says, quality cannot be inspected into a product or service. It must be designed in. The Ford Motor Company advertising slogan, "Quality is Job One," reflects this awareness.

Inputs

The earliest place to begin the control process is with the inputs to the transformation process. These typically include capital, labor, raw materials, and system design. In some situations, cost and availability of energy are also important inputs to the transformation system that need to be controlled. If the quality of the inputs is high, the chances for high-quality output are good. If the quality of inputs is low, the chances for high-quality output are essentially zero.

Steven Jobs, co-founder of Apple Computer and founder-CEO of Next Computer was quoted in the August 26, 1991 *Fortune* as saying, "Ultimately, I believe that most of the PCs [personal computers] will come from offshore. We're just not good enough at manufacturing." When the inputs available are not up to the necessary quality, proactive control would suggest the transformation process should not even begin.

Throughput

During the transformation process, many factors need to be controlled. Actual performance of machines, labor, management, and materials needs to be compared with standards. Work in progress can be tested for quality, training programs can be assessed for their effectiveness, and progress toward goals can be compared to the time remaining to reach the goals.

Output

Output controls are the easiest to measure. Unfortunately, they are the least helpful. Once an output or outcome exists, it can be counted, categorized, assessed, or measured. However, any problems discovered with it are already incorporated in the output. The money has already been spent.

Output controls focus on product or service quantity as well as quality. They also address timing—the product or service must be available when it is needed. The finest bid proposal in the world is not considered if it arrives six days late. Companies that produce consumer goods for the Christmas gift-giving season are under pressure in September and October to get their goods to market. Quantity, quality, and timing are all important control factors.

HOW TO MEASURE: METHODS

Once a standard has been set and a process or step has been identified as requiring control, the problem of how to measure actual performance arises.

Mechanical Measures

The simplest and most direct way is mechanically. For example, plastic extrusion molds (the technology which produces Frisbees and Rubbermaid products) can be used only for a certain number of pourings. With each pouring, a bit of the mold wears away, so the product gets successively larger. A simple mechanical counter tells when the mold requires replacement.

Cybernetic Systems

Cybernetic systems are self-feedback systems where a mechanical device adjusts a process to keep it controlled. The most common example is the thermostat on a home heater. Many other similar systems exist—basement sump pumps, for example, which shut off when water level is low and turn on when the water level rises.

The field of *psychocybernetics* studies automatic feedback loops as they apply in people or in computerized systems. The ability to self-adjust to changing system constraints makes for highly productive organizational members. However, in order for psychocybernetics to work, organizational members need a constant stream of information. As the last chapter mentioned, managers tent to resist sharing information with their subordinates.

Computers

Computers can easily be programmed to keep data on who is using them and what they are doing. Best Western Hotels have their computerized reservations center in Phoenix, Arizona. The company was keeping all kinds of data on each reservation clerk. Each 15 minutes, the reservation clerk with the highest number of calls taken would be announced. The constant measuring and competing resulted in high employee turnover. More recently Best Western's focus has turned from quantity to quality, and the computer's monitoring functions have been reduced.

Behavioral Measures

Behavioral performance is especially difficult to measure because so much of it is attitude. Even so, organizations try. At one new Bellevue, Washington club, The Lakes, the waiters are required to call each member by name four times per visit.

Special Techniques

Some situations require special measurement tools and techniques. These will be discussed in greater detail in chapter 21. Some situations require intuition and judgment in addition to measurement. For example, records are kept on dairy cattle that indicate number of gallons of milk they produce, percent fat, pounds of daily feed consumed, birth weights of calves, sexes of calves, days of milk production between calves and so on. When a cow's milk production falls to a certain level, she is removed from the herd. Or sometimes she is not. It depends. If a cow has daughters who are tremendous milk producers, it might be worth keeping her. Or if she has a calming effect on the other cows, perhaps her own lowered milk production is not as important. The herdskeeper must use experience and intuition to make a decision about what constitutes poor milk production.

MAKING CONTROL EFFECTIVE

People are very sensitive to the control process. When controls are too tight, too slack, or conflicting, certain symptoms are sure to arise. When a manager notices these symptomatic conditions, the process needs immediate attention.

Tight Controls

When people sense they are being too closely monitored, the following symptoms may be present.

Increased absenteeism and tardiness

Increased turnover

Declining morale

Inaccurate reporting of control data

Sabotage and theft of product and equipment

Slack Controls

Sometimes organizations get so busy handling the crises of the moment that the control system (like the planning system) is overlooked. Other times, a manager may not have the skills to discipline effectively and lets standards "slip." In these cases, the controls are too slack and need to be tightened up. The following symptoms are typical of too loose control.

Increased accidents

Disorder and dirt

Machine breakdowns

Excessive costs and waste

Customer complaints

Increased warranty claims

Poor quality and increased rework

Wrong Controls

Sometimes an organization's level of control is good, and what it is controlling is the wrong thing. The symptoms of this problem may take longer to arise and longer to cure. Some examples of wrong-control symptoms include the following.

Game playing. People may see controls as something to be beaten. Doing the minimum, padding the expense account, spending every penny in the budget are examples of control games. Control techniques can lose their effectiveness over time. Different controls or methods of measuring performance are required to reduce game playing. Peter Drucker said that he would not want workers who were too bored or dull to figure out a way around the rules! Once they do, the standards and the controls need to be reevaluated.

Conflicting goals. When marketers are asked to increase sales and decrease advertising, they may believe the control system has gone awry. If the credit department is tightening up its requirements for extending credit and the sales department is trying to increase sales, another conflict of goals is present.

Each of these symptoms can serve as feedback to the planning process. More careful attention is required to see that goals and controls are supportive of each other.

The ultimate purpose of controlling is the production of quality goods and services at a cost which reflects efficiency of operations. Overseeing the transformation process provides opportunities to correct problems before output has been affected. In spite of the importance of control, organizational members frequently resist what they perceive as limits to their freedom and creativity.

In some organizations, controls are too tight. Employees spend more time figuring out how to beat the controls than they do working to meet the standards. In such situations, the symptoms are usually obvious.

In a highly effective control system, many if not most of the controls are mechanical or cybernetic—they work quietly and unobtrusively in the background, they help rather than hinder; they provide information rather than punishment. The very best control system is well coordinated with the organization's goals and is proactive. It takes corrective action before crises occur.

Selected Readings

Anthony, R. N., J. Dearden, and N. M. Bedford. 1989. *Management Control Systems*. 6th ed. Homewood, IL: Irwin.

Campbell, David N., R. L. Fleming, and Richard C. Grote. 1985. "Discipline without Punishment—at Last." *Harvard Business Review* 63: 168.

Chew, W. Bruce. 1988. "No-Nonsense Guide to Measuring Productivity." *Harvard Business Review* 66: 110–119.

Green, Stephen G., and M. Ann Welsh. 1988. "Cybernetics and Dependence: Reframing the Control Concept." *Academy of Management Review* 13: 287–301.

Jaeger, A. M., and B. R. Baliga. 1985. "Control Systems and Strategic Adaptation: Lessons from the Japanese Experience." *Strategic Management Journal* 6: 115–134.

Latham, G. P., and G. A. Yukl. 1975. "A Review of Research on the Application of Goal Setting in Organizations." *Academy of Management Journal* 18: 824–829.

Walton, Richard E. 1985. "From Control to Commitment in the Workplace." *Harvard Business Review* 63: 77–84.

Index